HER MAJESTY
QUEEN ELIZABETH II

THIS BOOK IS DEDICATED
TO
THE STAFF AND PUPILS OF
GREAT CHART COUNTY PRIMARY SCHOOL, KENT
If only all children could attend a school this wonderful

First published in the United States in 2012 by Running Press Book Publishers, A Member of the Perseus Books Group

First published in the UK in 2012 by Constable, an imprint of Constable & Robinson Ltd,
in association with *The Daily Mail*

Copyright © 2012 text, Michael Paterson Copyright © photographs (unless otherwise stated) *Daily Mail*

All rights reserved under the Pan-American and International Copyright Conventions

This book may not be reproduced in whole or in part, in any form or by any means, electronic or mechanical, including photocopying, recording, or by any information storage and retrieval system now known or hereafter invented, without written permission from the publisher.

Books published by Running Press are available at special discounts for bulk purchases in the United States by corporations, institutions, and other organizations. For more information, please contact the Special Markets Department at the Perseus Books Group, 2300 Chestnut Street, Suite 200, Philadelphia, PA 19103, or call (800) 810-4145, ext. 5000, or e-mail special.markets@perseusbooks.com.

US ISBN 978-0-7624-4645-2
US Library of Congress Control Number: 2011943776

9 8 7 6 5 4 3 2 1
Digit on the right indicates the number of this printing

Running Press Book Publishers
2300 Chestnut Street
Philadelphia, PA 19103-4371

Visit us on the web!
www.runningpress.com

Designed by D23, London
Printed in Italy

All photographs supplied from the Daily Mail Photo Archive except for the following:
Rex Features – Pages 4, 6/7, 8(top), 16(top right), 24(bottom), 30(middle and bottom left), 42(middle right, bottom), 60, 74/75, 76, 92, 96/97, 98, 118/119, 159(top), 171, 172 (top), 183(top right), 186(top). Corbis – 20, 23, 24(top left), 27, 28, 29, 30(top), 33(bottom right), 36/37, 42(top right and left), 45, 54/55, 56, 63(bottom), 64(top left). Press Association – 41, 63(top), 87, 88, 91(bottom left), 95(bottom), 120(bottom left), 128(top), 131, 132(top and bottom right), 136(bottom), 148(top right), 163, 164(top), 165/166, 172(bottom), 175(left), 176(middle right and bottom), 179, 180(top), 183(top left and bottom), 187, 188(top), 189(top), 190(top right and bottom), 192. Daily Herald – 16(top left). Imperial War Museum – 18/19.

HER MAJESTY
QUEEN ELIZABETH II

DIAMOND JUBILEE
1952 – 2012

MICHAEL PATERSON

RUNNING PRESS
PHILADELPHIA · LONDON

Queen Elizabeth II is the most famous woman in the world. Because of the multitude of positions she holds, the influence she wields, the world leaders she has known and – most significantly – the length of time she has been in the public eye, she outdistances any competition. Others have undoubtedly wielded political power or social influence, but their exposure on the world stage has been brief, seldom more than a decade or so. That greatly overrated quality, 'celebrity,' is even more fickle and short-lived.

The Queen is not a celebrity, and hates any notion of herself or her family possessing glamour or 'star quality.' These things are not what the Royal Family is about. The Queen is not there to start fashion trends, to take up current fads, to reflect the views of the moment. Even as an undoubtedly beautiful young sovereign, she had no interest in courting photographers or showing off her wardrobe. Such behaviour is, and always was, beneath her dignity. Her Majesty, and the rest of the Royal Family, are there to reflect the long-term, timeless values of the nation and the Commonwealth. They do not seek publicity or exposure. They prefer to be dutiful, predictable, reassuringly familiar and, if necessary, dull. They are a symbol of stability, a relative constant in a world that never ceases to undergo rapid change.

As will be seen from the pictures in this book the Queen has, for much of her reign, personified this timelessness. The style of her clothes has not changed significantly since the 1960s (though her hats are very different – they tend now to be flat-topped and wide-brimmed). Her hairstyle, similarly, has been the same for almost fifty years as, in the interests of continuity, it must remain exactly as it is on stamps and coins.

Whatever the position into which the Queen was born, she could not have fulfilled her duties so well had she not had a temperament suited to the task. Surrounded by good example and good advice, she followed both. She has been comfortable with her position. She is by nature thorough, conscientious and reliant on routine – thriving on the very thing that others might consider tedious and restricting. She enjoys what she does, and knows she does it well.

She has never abused her position, or put her own wishes before her duty. She has never been guilty of favouritism, political partisanship or financial irregularity. Apart from not wearing a hard hat when riding, she is blameless in public and in private.

It is a certainty that she will rank in history with the great female sovereigns: Catherine the Great, Maria Theresa, Queen Victoria, and the first Elizabeth. The latter two were her childhood heroines. It must surely afford her some satisfaction to know that she is as great a queen as they were.

CHAPTER ONE: 1926–1939

❧

CHILDHOOD OF A MONARCH

PREVIOUS SPREAD: One of the earliest known photographs of Princess Elizabeth, 1926.

TOP: The Christening of Princess Elizabeth Alexandra Mary, Buckingham Palace, May 1926. From left to right – Lady Elphinstone (aunt/godmother); Arthur, duke of Connaught (great-great-uncle/godfather); Queen Mary; King George V; the Duchess of York (holding her daughter); the Duke of York; the Countess and Earl of Strathmore (maternal grandparents, Earl also godparent); Princess Mary (aunt/godmother).

BOTTOM LEFT: Princess Elizabeth with Queen Mary, Charlotte (King's parrot) and Snip (King's terrier), Balmoral, 1928.

BOTTOM RIGHT: Princess Elizabeth with her grandfather, King George V, Balmoral, 1928.

Running westward from Bond Street to Berkeley Square, Bruton Street is in the midst of London's Mayfair. Today it is associated with the galleries of clothing designers, whose names appear on their shopfronts. Not a single private house remains.

Number 17 is now a very modern office block but eighty years ago, on this site, stood the town house of the Earl of Strathmore. He was the maternal grandfather of Princess Elizabeth, and it was here that she was born by Caesarean section on 21 April 1926, at 2:40 a.m.

Her father was Albert ('Bertie') Duke of York, second son of King George V. Her mother was the former Elizabeth Bowes-Lyon, a member of an illustrious Scottish noble family.

Princess Elizabeth was not heir to the throne, but she was the first grandchild within the immediate Royal Family.

The princess was christened, five weeks after birth, by the Archbishop of Canterbury in the chapel at Buckingham Palace, wrapped in the same Honiton lace garment as had been used for her father, grandfather and great-grandfather. The names chosen for her – Elizabeth Alexandra Mary – referred to her mother, great-grandmother (who had just died) and grandmother.

The baby princess was separated from her parents when the Duke and Duchess went on an official tour to Australia. They missed her first birthday as a result. Her time was divided between her Strathmore relations, and the King and Queen. The King had terrified his sons and grandsons, but took at once to this little girl, whom he spoiled. He liked to have breakfast with Elizabeth and to take her to see the horses at his stud. The seeds of a lifetime's passion were sown here.

When her parents returned from overseas the little princess appeared with them on the palace balcony as they acknowledged the cheers of the crowd. It was her first public appearance. The Duke and Duchess had been presented on their travels with no less than three tons of toys for her. She received a few of them, but the great majority were given to children in hospital.

The young princess invented for herself the name by which she has been known to intimates ever since. 'Lilibet' was her early attempt to enunciate her own name, and somehow it stuck. More than 80 years later, she still uses it when signing Christmas cards to relatives and old friends.

On 21 August, 1930, Princess Elizabeth's sister, Princess Margaret, was born. The girls grew to be very close, partly because they did not go to school and their circumstances made it difficult for them to make friends. The girls looked very similar, both having the same chin-length chestnut hair and blue eyes, and were always dressed, if not the same, then at least similarly but they had quite different personalities. Elizabeth was earnest, conscientious and eager to please. Margaret was comical, wilful, irreverent and mischievous, a gifted singer and mimic who loved performing. Elizabeth had a temper inherited from her father and grandfather, but this was not often seen. She disliked confrontation and would let her sister have her way to avoid it.

Like her sister, Elizabeth could also amuse grown-ups. At Sandringham the Archbishop of Canterbury once asked if she would walk with him in the garden. She agreed, but stipulated: 'Please do not tell me anything more about God. I know all about Him already.' Such remarks caused her grandmother to introduce her as 'Princess Elizabeth, who hopes one day to be a lady.'

The family had two homes. In London they lived at 145 Piccadilly, a mansion house with windows looking towards the gardens of Buckingham Palace. The house was destroyed by wartime bombing. The girls lived on the top floor, where a large glass dome shed light on the stairwell. Beneath this, on the landing, they kept an extensive and neatly ordered collection of toy horses, all of which were groomed and exercised.

The other, weekend, home of the Yorks was White Lodge in Richmond Park. Stuck in the midst of parkland that was entirely accessible to the public, it was inconvenient and lacked privacy. Only

TOP LEFT: Princess Elizabeth chats with the Dowager, Countess of Airlie, 1931.

TOP RIGHT: Princess Elizabeth playing in the summerhouse in the garden of 145 Piccadilly.

BOTTOM: With her mother, grandmother and Prince George at the Trooping the Colour in 1931, celebrating the King's 66th birthday.

in 1932 did they escape to a more secluded house – Royal Lodge in Windsor Great Park. Within a short distance of Royal Lodge was built the Wendy house of every small girl's dreams. 'Y Bwthyn Bach' ('the little house' in Welsh) was a gift from the people of the principality on Elizabeth's sixth birthday. The roof of this two-storey building was thatched (it still has to be renewed periodically), and the rooms (which are too small for adults to stand up in) were fully equipped with working lights, running water and miniature versions of household implements – from a dustpan to a vacuum cleaner and a radio. Elizabeth could be as fastidious in her sweeping and cleaning as her tidy nature desired.

The duke and duchess were indulgent with their daughters and saw the girls for at least an hour, twice a day, usually also taking their meals together. Once they were old enough for school, there was no thought of sending them away as boarders. Not only was there no family precedent for such a move, but the King and Queen were simply not willing to part with them. Queen Mary devised a curriculum. She considered it unnecessary for them to learn much about arithmetic, since there would be little need for that. They must, of course, have a great deal of history, as well as knowing something of current affairs. In addition to *The Children's Newspaper*, they therefore read *Punch*, and *The Times*.

Their governess, appointed in 1933, was Miss Marion Crawford. A Scot, she was nicknamed 'Crawfie' by Elizabeth. She was to stay with the girls throughout their upbringing and to spend the war years with them at Windsor.

Riding continued to be the girls' passion as they progressed from toy horses to real ones. At the age of four, Elizabeth was taught to ride on the orders of King George by his stud-groom. The child was a very willing pupil, regarding her teacher, Owen, with respectful awe. She rapidly acquired a detailed knowledge of tack, saddlery and feed, things that became her chief topic of conversation.

The princesses' family life was shattered, suddenly, when their

TOP: Trooping the Colour, June 1935, Princess Elizabeth practises the 'Royal Wave' with Queen Mary while Princess Margaret and the girls' mother look on.

LEFT: Princess Elizabeth on her way to the circus at Olympia with her mother, 1934.

MIDDLE RIGHT: 'The Little House' at the *Daily Mail* Ideal Home Exhibition at Olympia, 1932.

BOTTOM RIGHT: The Duke and Duchess of York enjoying 'The Little House' with their daughters and pets.

Uncle David abdicated the throne on 10 December 1936. They discovered the full implications of the crisis only on the day that their father succeeded his brother. Elizabeth saw in the hall a letter left for 'Her Majesty the Queen' and asked: 'That's Mummy now, isn't it?'

The family moved to Buckingham Palace. Although no generation of Royals seems to like the palace, no child could inherit such a kingdom and be unimpressed. There were lengthy corridors – on which they could ride their tricycles – mysterious stairs, cellars and an entire inner quadrangle. The girls lined up their equine toys in the passageway outside their second-floor suite of rooms, although the King had their rocking horse put outside his study so that he could hear the sounds of his children romping.

Once the duke became King, Elizabeth's position naturally also changed. She was now first in line to the throne. Now she was to be schooled specifically for her future tasks.

The King himself took on the task of instructing Elizabeth in the performance of a monarch's duties, and a famous photograph, taken when Elizabeth was aged 16, captures this passing on of experience. It shows the King at his desk with his daughter looking over his shoulder as he explains a document from his dispatch box.

Knowing that his eldest daughter might well experience her own coronation within a decade or two, the King used his coronation in May 1937 to teach her about the ceremony, its participants and its significance. He had a picture book created that showed the event from beginning to end, and went through it with her.

Elizabeth had already, as a small girl, learned how to wave to crowds. Gradually, during the 1930s, she had become more noticeable at Royal occasions. She was a bridesmaid at the wedding of her uncle, the Duke of Kent, in 1934. She participated in the celebrations for her grandfather's Silver Jubilee. In May 1937, she and Margaret attended their father's coronation in Westminster Abbey wearing identical crowns.

Elizabeth was encouraged to write a journal of the event, and she

TOP LEFT: The King's coach at Admiralty Arch during his coronation procession, 12 May 1937.

TOP RIGHT: Lady Mary Cambridge (10) and Princess Elizabeth (8) were bridesmaids when the Duke of York married Princess Marina of Greece and Denmark in 1934.

MIDDLE: On the balcony at Buckingham Palace, the princesses celebrate the marriage of their Uncle Henry, Duke of Gloucester, to Lady Alice Christabel Montagu Douglas Scott, November 1935.

BOTTOM RIGHT: Princess Elizabeth and Princess Margaret, leave Westminster Abbey following their father's coronation.

BOTTOM LEFT: The royal family on the balcony at Buckingham Palace after the coronation of King George VI.

did so with characteristic thoroughness. On lined paper she wrote neatly in pencil: 'The Coronation, 12 May 1937. To Mummy and Papa. From Lilibet By Herself.' It is preserved in the Royal Archives.

Soon afterwards, her education took a further step forward. It was arranged that she should take lessons in constitutional history from the Vice Provost of Eton. Henry Marten was amiably professorial, charming and extremely capable. The Princess visited him twice weekly in company with Miss Crawford. They sat in his untidy, book-filled study, where he kept a tame raven. The heir to the throne received one-to-one tuition specifically tailored to her own circumstances from a man who was perhaps the most gifted history teacher of his generation.

Elizabeth was aged 13 when, in the summer of 1939, she experienced one of the most significant moments in her life. On 22 June she visited Britannia Royal Naval College at Dartmouth with her parents and sister. They arrived aboard the Royal Yacht, *Victoria and Albert*. A young cadet, Prince Philip of Greece, the nephew of the king's cousin, 'Dickie' Mountbatten, was instructed to entertain them and when the visit came to an end, *Victoria and Albert* steamed out of Dartmouth Harbour accompanied by a fleet of small craft manned by members of the college. Most turned back once in the choppier waters of the open sea, but a single boat continued to follow until Philip — for it was he — had to be ordered by loud-hailer to return. Elizabeth was deeply impressed by Philip's handsome appearance and his brash self-confidence. In the months and years that followed she fell seriously in love with him.

TOP LEFT: Princess Elizabeth has her belt adjusted watched by her father and sister during a Girl Guides parade at Windsor Castle, 1938.

TOP RIGHT: Princesses Margaret and Elizabeth salute the parade in a colourized photograph.

BOTTOM LEFT: The young princesses were often dressed identically as here in 1939.

BOTTOM RIGHT: Princess Elizabeth, resplendent in a flowered hat at the Aldershot Tattoo, 1938.

CHAPTER TWO: 1939 –1947

❦

THE
WAR YEARS

On the outbreak of war, in September 1939, the princesses were at Balmoral, and remained there. In London there were air raid drills, wardens and auxiliary medical services, concrete shelters and sandbags everywhere. It was speculated that the princesses might go to Canada to wait out hostilities. King George would not consider this. He would not be parted from his daughters, and saw it as important to national morale that the Royal Family stay in Britain.

The girls would live at Royal Lodge for the time being, where they would be safe enough from aerial attack. The King and Queen lived largely at Buckingham Palace, feeling that it was important to remain in the capital. They spoke to the princesses by telephone at six o'clock every evening but saw them only at weekends, which they spent at Windsor. Both the sovereign and his consort practiced shooting with rifles and pistols and, when travelling, the King sometimes carried a sten gun. Should the Germans invade, the Queen declared that: 'I shall not go down like the others.' The monarchies of Belgium and Denmark were trapped by the invaders when German forces overran western Europe in May 1940. Those of Norway and the Netherlands had to flee. The British monarchy was determined to fight. Even Queen Mary toted a pistol.

And there were some dangerous moments. In September 1940, two days after the start of the Blitz, a bomb fell on Buckingham Palace. It did not explode and the King carried on working in his study above it. It did blow up the next day, destroying the swimming-pool that had only recently been built. While this attack might have been random, there was another one exactly a week later that was intentional. The palace was extremely conspicuous from the air, and a raider flew calmly up The Mall to drop a total of six bombs, which landed in the forecourt, the quadrangle, the chapel and the garden.

Meanwhile, the girls helped collect scrap metal for the war effort and, like all children living in the country at that time, they helped with the harvesting of fruit and vegetables. They made donations

PREVIOUS SPREAD: Princess Elizabeth, aged 18, served as a junior officer in the Auxiliary Territorial Service, 1945.

LEFT: Princesses Elizabeth and Margaret with Jane, the corgi, Windsor Castle, 1940.

from their pocket money to help the Red Cross. Elizabeth made a gallant attempt to knit items of clothing for soldiers – this was something the aged Queen Victoria had done during the Boer War – but the experiment was not a success.

After the fall of France in the summer of 1940, there was a real possibility of German invasion. The girls were moved for safety from Royal Lodge into the castle itself. Isolated on its hilltop amid extensive grounds, it was almost impossible for enemy bombers to miss had they made a serious attempt. On a number of occasions the sirens sent them down to the castle's dungeons, one of which had been prepared as a shelter. The first time this happened, there was sudden concern when the princesses and their nanny failed to appear. Sir Hill Child, the Master of the Household, was beside himself with anxiety. Miss Crawford, the governess called up the stair of the Brunswick Tower, in which the girls had their quarters: 'What are you doing?'

'We're dressing,' replied Elizabeth.

Child made it clear that in future there must be no such delays. With practice a routine was established. The girls had bunks in the shelter, suitcases packed with both essentials and sentimental treasures, and 'siren-suits' – as popularised by the Prime Minister – to enable them to be dressed in seconds.

Against this background of enemy action, the 34-member Buckingham Palace Guide Troop had transferred to Windsor where they carried on their activities, though now they were drilled by a Sergeant Major of the Grenadiers. They held a camp in the park, but this was no ordinary troop – their tents were erected for them by guardsmen and their food was provided by the castle pantries. Elizabeth, with her trademark shyness already in evidence, found excuse to sleep on her own in a nearby summer house rather than under canvas.

On 13 October, 1940, Princess Elizabeth, then fourteen, broadcast to the children of the Empire on the radio programme *Children's Hour*. Coached in delivery, and with her mother beating time, the Princess said in a measured and confident voice: 'My sister Margaret Rose and I

TOP LEFT: Elizabeth and Margaret with Chung at the Royal Lodge, Windsor, 1942.

TOP RIGHT: The princesses as Girl Guides, with Elizabeth practising putting Margaret's arm in a sling, Frogmore, Windsor, 1942.

BOTTOM: Princess Elizabeth makes her first broadcast, October 1940.

feel so much for you, for we too know from experience what it means to be away from those we love most of all.' She ended on an upbeat: 'We know, every one of us, that in the end all shall be well.' Princess Margaret, at her elbow, joined her in wishing her audience farewell: 'Good night, and good luck to you all.' It was a well-delivered speech that has remained fixed in the national memory. Together with the talk she was to broadcast on her twenty-first birthday, it was among the most memorable of all the hundreds the Queen has given.

Windsor was a most agreeable place in which to sit out these years of confinement. There were interesting and talented people wherever one looked. Sir Hill Child may have wrung his hands over the princesses' slowness in dressing, but he also showed them the castle cellars where the Crown Jewels were hidden, wrapped in newspaper. There were also local teachers helping to maintain morale. Hubert Tanner was headmaster of the little local school in the park and produced, for Christmas 1940, a nativity play that was performed by local children, evacuees and . . . the princesses. Both girls delighted in the experience, and the following year a more ambitious undertaking was attempted. This was a pantomime – *Cinderella* – with sophisticated costumes, and original music by Mr Tanner (who also acted in the productions) that was staged in the castle's Waterloo Chamber. It perhaps goes without saying that the two princesses had the lead roles – but then a major purpose was to train the girls toward confidence in public – with Elizabeth as Prince Charming and her sister as Cinderella. The audience was local people, estate workers, soldiers and the families of castle staff. The King, who had a simple and hearty sense of humour, laughed loudly throughout. His own shyness having never left him, he was gratified to see that his heir could appear in public with such lack of inhibition.

The performances became an annual tradition. *Aladdin* was put on the next year, and was followed by a show whose title – *Old Mother Red Riding Boots* – suggests a rather tongue-in-cheek concoction based on several children's stories. For the princesses these productions,

TOP LEFT: Princess Elizabeth in *Old Mother Red Riding Boots*, 1944.

TOP RIGHT: Elizabeth as Prince Charming and Margaret as Cinderella, January 1942.

BOTTOM: Hubert Tanner with an unknown cast member, Princess Elizabeth and Princess Margaret in *Aladdin*, 1943.

with their elaborate costumes and serving soldiers drafted in as extras, were an important part of their lives. A frisson of excitement was added during *Aladdin* by the presence in the audience of Philip, on leave from the navy.

Further afield, the Royal Family lost its first member on active service for centuries. Prince George, Duke of Kent, the King's youngest surviving brother had been serving in the RAF. Elizabeth had been a bridesmaid at his wedding in 1934. He was tragically killed not in action but in a flying accident. Wartime air travel was highly risky. The King, on two occasions, flew overseas to visit theatres of operations. Both times he returned without mishap.

The King was well aware that, by courting danger, he was increasing the risk that his daughter might suddenly become Queen, and she must be as prepared as possible. She was, in any case, reaching young adulthood and it would not be long before she began to assume some royal duties. For the time being, her only official position was that of Sea Ranger. She had graduated to this after passing out of the Guides on reaching sixteen. On her birthday that year she went, as did all young women of her age, to a Labour Exchange to register for work under the Wartime Youth Service Scheme. She longed to do something useful, and relished having this experience in common with others of her age, but it was no more than a gesture. The King refused to let her be assigned any form of duty, believing that she was already helping the war effort by keeping up morale through her membership of the Royal Family. He found her an appointment that was more suitable.

Her father appointed Princess Elizabeth Colonel of the Grenadier Guards. She took the salute at a parade on her birthday as the youngest-ever Colonel-in-Chief in the British Army but there was nothing schoolgirlish about her attitude. At the parade she stood ramrod-straight and solemn-faced, and when inspecting the men found fault with details to such an extent that she had to be tactfully asked to show less zeal.

RIGHT: Princess Elizabeth in her Sea Ranger uniform, 1944.

FOLLOWING PAGES
LEFT: The Royal Family and Chung, 1946.

RIGHT: Princess Elizabeth at Buckingham Palace, 1946.

And it was at this same age that she discovered the pleasures of racing. She was taken by the King to Wiltshire to watch his trainer exercising horses on the downs. She met a jockey – Gordon Richards – and was introduced to a world of equine specialists and experts whose manner, and speech, and knowledge she found fascinating. She was, remarkably quickly, to match their expertise. She visited the Royal Stud soon afterwards, establishing a connection that has continued ever since. Her father had been a nominal race-goer; his daughter would make up for his lack of fervour.

Though devoted to her parents and willing to be guided by her elders, Elizabeth possessed a good deal of stubbornness. By the beginning of 1945 the conflict, in Europe at least, was clearly not going to last much longer. She still longed for an active role in the war effort and badgered her father to grant his permission to enlist. He eventually yielded and allowed her to join the Armed Forces. Elizabeth joined the ATS – Auxiliary Territorial Service – and was to be proud for the rest of her life of the mechanical and driving skills it gave her. She was commissioned as Second Subaltern (lieutenant) Princess Elizabeth, Army number 20873, and attached to No. 1 Mechanical Transport Training Centre near Camberley – a place sufficiently near Windsor to make commuting possible. She was fitted for her khaki uniform, and polished the buttons herself!

The princess, however, did not share all the experiences of her contemporaries. On the first day of service she was collected from Windsor by her commanding officer. Thereafter, at the insistence of the King, she returned home every evening to dine and sleep. Though she shared the duties of her unit, acting as officer of the day when her turn came, she did not mingle with the others. At lectures she came into the room last and left it first, always occupying the middle of the front row and flanked by senior officers. No one addressed her as anything other than Ma'am or Your Royal Highness, though the girls had little chance to talk to her anyway. Yet she was as curious about them as they must have been about her. Whenever one of them asked

TOP: The Royal Family in the garden at the Royal Lodge, Windsor, 1946.

MIDDLE LEFT: Princess Elizabeth with a working horse at Sandringham, 1944.

MIDDLE RIGHT: The Princesses leaving the wedding of Lady Anne Spencer and Lieutenant Christopher Baldwin Hughes Wake-Walker at Westminster Abbey, February 1944.

BOTTOM LEFT: Princess Elizabeth training with the ATS, 1945.

BOTTOM RIGHT: The princesses purchase the first two £1 issue Saving Certificates at a Post Office in January 1943.

a question in a lecture, the Princess would turn in her seat and stare at them, anxious to recognise faces and learn names. A rare and useful glimpse of Royalty from the other side was afforded her, however, when she had to help prepare the camp for a visit by the Princess Royal, her aunt. She later fumed: 'What a business it has been. Spit and polish all day long. Now I know what goes on when Mummy and Papa go anywhere.'

She completed the course in vehicle maintenance, but in the process she had become obsessed with technicalities. 'We had sparking-plugs last night all through dinner,' her mother famously sighed. The King and Queen attended her graduation, and no doubt were as proud as she was.

As well as learning to repair engines, the princess perfected her ability to drive. She had already taken lessons in Windsor Great Park, and had been given a Daimler by the King for her eighteenth birthday. She took her test by driving her commanding officer to Buckingham Palace from Aldershot.

She began to take a structured, rather than occasional, part in public duties. She acted as hostess to visiting military and political leaders, visited camps and bases, inspected troops, and even travelled in secret to watch a rehearsal for the parachute drop that would take place on D-day.

As evidence that she had now joined the adult world, Elizabeth was given her own rooms in Buckingham Palace – a bedroom, dressing-room, bathroom and sitting-room that overlooked The Mall. She was also given two members of staff – a housemaid and footman. Within a few months of her birthday she was to perform the duty of Councillor of State, signing the reprieve for a murderer. She would also attend a luncheon at Guildhall and make a public speech for the first time.

When the war ended in Europe, Elizabeth joined her parents, and the Prime Minister, on the palace balcony on the 8 May, dressed in her khaki ATS uniform. After dark, with the celebrations still going

TOP LEFT: Princess Elizabeth at her first Charity Ball in the Dorchester, May 1946, dancing with Captain Lord Rupert Nevill who later became Private Secretary to Prince Philip.

TOP RIGHT: The princess dancing at the Royal Caledonian Ball in Grosvenor House, June 1946.

BOTTOM RIGHT: The heir to the throne is given an understanding of her responsibilities while watching her father at work, Windsor, 1942.

BOTTOM LEFT: Princess Elizabeth and General Montgomery watch an England versus Scotland football match at Wembley, 24 February 1944. Monty can be forgiven for looking stressed as it was only 3 months before D-Day. England won 6-2.

on, Elizabeth and Margaret persuaded the King to let them out into the crowd. Once suitable escorts were arranged, he gave consent. After dark, she and Margaret went, with several friends and young officers as escort, incognito into the crowd. They went along The Mall into Piccadilly Circus, unrecognised. They also stood in front of the palace and joined in the calls for the King and Queen. Their parents knew they would be somewhere outside in the sea of faces, and had been told they must appear!

Three months later the scene was repeated when Japan surrendered. This time Elizabeth stood on the balcony not in uniform but in a summer dress, and she filmed the crowds with a movie camera.

With the war over and the princess now grown up, there was naturally speculation about whom she would marry. The King was concerned that his daughter had not met enough young men to make a mature judgment regarding her future, but there could be no questioning her affection for Prince Philip. She had kept his photograph on her desk for years and written to him frequently. He had served in the Mediterranean, where his ship bombarded the Libyan coast and took part in the battle at Cape Matapan. In this action, which had put Italy's surface fleet out of the war, he had manned the searchlights aboard *HMS Valiant*. He was given a Mention in Dispatches that read: 'Thanks to his alertness and appreciation of the situation, we were able to sink in five minutes two Italian cruisers.' He took part in convoys along the east coast of Britain. He crossed the Atlantic, and he was posted to the Pacific. In between, however, he had appeared in London several times on leave. Elizabeth was clearly delighted to see him. No one could have mistaken her excitement when she found he was coming to *Aladdin* at Windsor. Though they had not been together a great deal, they had seen enough of each other to deepen their friendship significantly.

TOP LEFT: The Queen and her daughters attending a charity concert at the Royal Opera House in Covent Garden, February 1946.

TOP RIGHT: Princess Elizabeth on her way to launch the new aircraft carrier HMS *Eagle*, March 1946.

BOTTOM LEFT: Princess Elizabeth and Margaret at a Girl Guide and Rangers rally in Hyde Park, May 1946.

BOTTOM RIGHT: Princess Elizabeth with Lieutenant Mountbatten, September 1946.

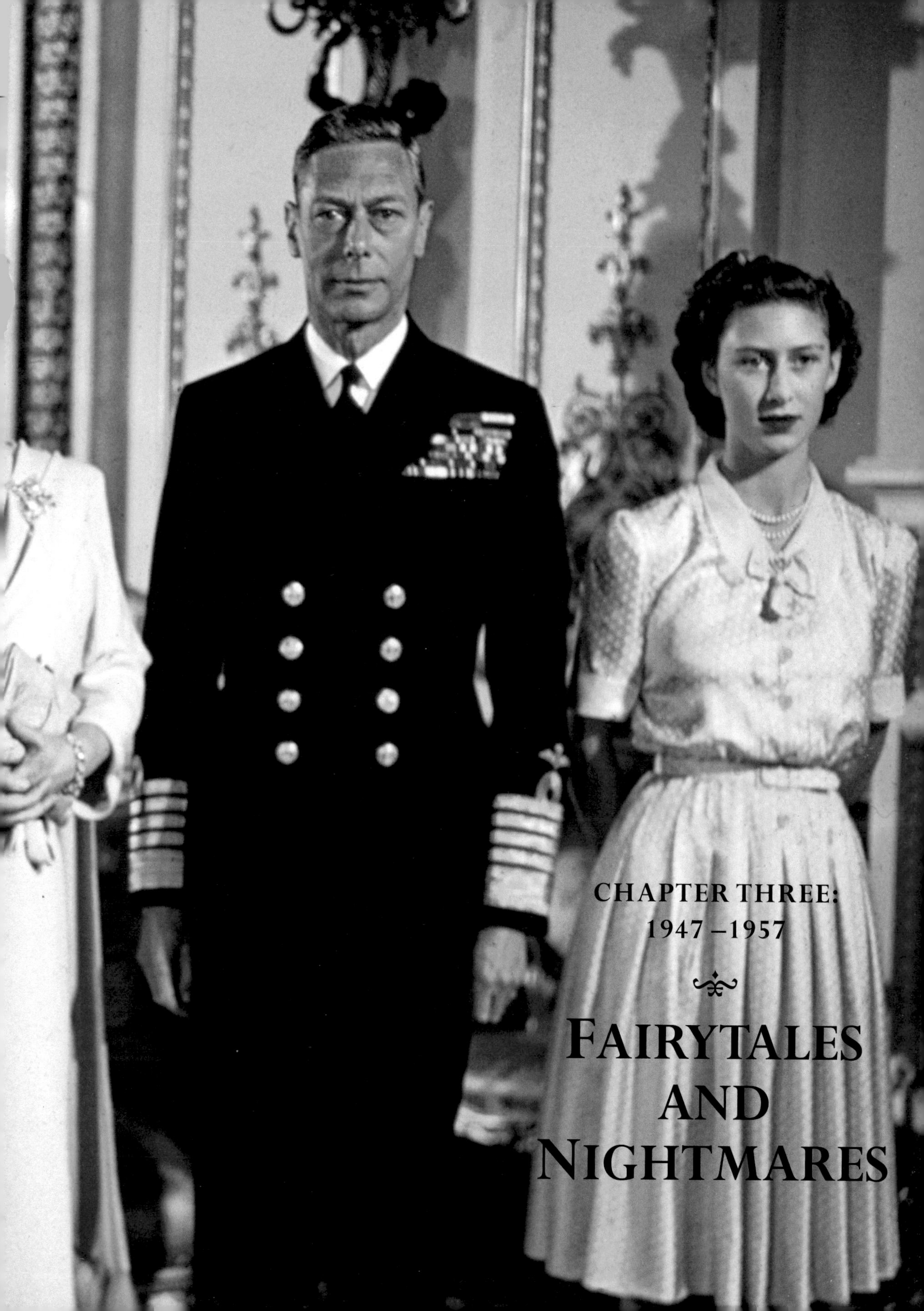

CHAPTER THREE:
1947 –1957

FAIRYTALES AND NIGHTMARES

With the war over, Princess Elizabeth's public duties became more routine. She now visited towns and factories rather than camps or troops in training, often carrying out these functions with her parents or her grandmother.

She had by now taken on the patronage, or presidency, of several organisations: the RSPCC, the Royal College of Music, the Life Saving Society, the Red Cross, the Student Nurses' Association. She already spent her days answering letters, accepting – or declining – invitations, attending lunches, and making speeches.

Her shyness endeared her to her father's subjects but the matter about which she felt most reticent was Philip. Her feelings for him had not changed, and her determination to marry him was obvious. The King still had difficulty in accepting that she had fallen for him so quickly. His uncle, Lord Mountbatten, was persistent in pushing his suit. He had been at Dartmouth on the day of the Royal Family's visit, and it was he who had arranged for Philip to look after the girls.

The princess obviously liked Philip but her mother was less impressed. The Queen distrusted Mountbatten, and his sponsorship of Philip did not stand in the young man's favour. Even the candidate himself became alarmed by the vigour with which his uncle seemed to be forcing matters, pleading in a letter: 'Please, I beg of you, not too much advice in an affair of the heart or I shall be forced to do the wooing by proxy.'

Philip was the nephew of a marquess – Milford Haven – but showed none of the quiet urbanity that was the ideal of the aristocracy. He had been to a British boarding school but it was not the kind of traditional, top-drawer establishment that would have been taken seriously by courtiers. He obviously had a rebellious streak and it was wondered, given his striking looks, overwhelming confidence and popularity, whether he would be able to resist temptation enough to remain a faithful husband.

The British public proved surprisingly reluctant to take to him.

PREVIOUS SPREAD: The Royal Family at Buckingham Palace following the announcement of Princess Elizabeth's engagement to Lieutenant Mountbatten.

TOP: Princess Elizabeth and Princess Margaret meeting midshipmen aboard HMS *Anson* in the Clyde, July 1947.

BOTTOM: Princess Elizabeth, in a dark blue uniform, follows her father accompanied by the Duke of Gloucester for the Trooping the Colour ceremony, June 1947.

Once he had been seen in public with the princess – the first occasion was the wedding of Patricia Mountbatten – the press began to speculate openly. As the question of an engagement hovered, there remained a feeling that Elizabeth could do better. However handsome he might be, whatever his war record, Philip was seen as a foreigner.

In the autumn of 1946, Philip was invited to Balmoral. The purpose of his stay there was, at least partly, to give him a thorough vetting as to his suitability for life in the Royal Family. He was keen on outdoor pursuits, and adapted without difficulty to the shooting-and-stalking culture of Deeside. Philip and Elizabeth became engaged at some point during those weeks. Yet there was no public announcement. The King wanted to delay the news until after a visit to South Africa early in 1947.

All four members of the immediate Royal Family were to go, and they would be away for four months. Elizabeth once more took exception to the wishes of her parents but, despite her stubbornness, she gave way.

Why was the King so intent on secrecy? First of all, Elizabeth was not yet 21, and the King wanted her to have passed that milestone before her engagement was made public. Secondly, the man she wished to marry was not a British citizen, although he was in the process of becoming naturalised.

Furthermore, the King wanted to be sure that Elizabeth was certain. Because of her high public profile there could be no mistakes. He wanted his daughter to have several months in which to search her heart and see if her fondness was genuine. Once the family was home a decision could be made.

For the visit to South Africa, Elizabeth and Margaret were given an allotment of extra clothing coupons. Wartime rationing was still in place, but it was expected that Royals always be immaculate. One formal dress each would not have sufficed. They sailed aboard HMS *Vanguard*, the Royal Navy's largest battleship. Elizabeth knew the ship, having attended its launch as it was prepared for the expected invasion of Japan.

RIGHT: Princess Elizabeth preferred the young Lieutenant Mountbatten without his beard.

In April, the princess celebrated her 21st birthday. Her hosts, the government of South Africa, presented her with a necklace of 21 diamonds – which she was shortly to wear at her wedding. She marked the occasion by making the second important radio address of her life, and she prepared for it with customary diligence. She wrote the rough draft during a day's relaxation on the coast while the King and Princess Margaret swam in the sea. Later, aboard the royal train, she rehearsed the speech with her sister as audience. It was very simple: 'I declare before you all that my whole life, whether it be long or short, shall be devoted to your service and the service of the great Imperial Commonwealth to which we all belong. But I shall not have strength to carry out this resolution unless you join in it with me, as I now invite you to do. I know that your support will be unfailingly given. God bless all of you who are willing to share it.'

When the Royals arrived home, Philip was forbidden to appear among the welcoming party, for his presence would have sent an immediate signal to the public. Still living on his naval officer's pay, he had been saving up for an engagement ring, but in the event his mother provided the necessary jewels from family sources, including her own ring. The result was an arrangement with a solitaire diamond that had five smaller diamonds each side, set in platinum. The princess was given this at the beginning of July and wore it from then on. The wedding ring itself would not prove a financial burden, for the people of Wales donated one made from Welsh gold.

The date was set for 20 November 1947. It was felt by both the palace and the government that the wedding should take place at St George's Chapel, Windsor. The country was still in a process of painful economic recovery from the war, and a low-key ceremony was considered in keeping with the times. It quickly became clear, however, that Parliament and the Royal Family had misread the national mood. After years of drabness and hardship the public longed to have spectacle again. The ceremony was quickly replanned for Westminster Abbey.

TOP RIGHT: The diamond necklace presented to Princess Elizabeth from the people of South Africa for her 21st birthday, 1947.

TOP LEFT: Princess Elizabeth plays tag with midshipmen aboard HMS *Vanguard* en route to South Africa, February 1947.

MIDDLE RIGHT: Princess Elizabeth celebrates her 21st birthday in South Africa, 21 April 1947.

BOTTOM: The princesses riding on the beach in South Africa, 1947.

For her dress, Princess Elizabeth was granted a hundred additional clothing coupons, while each of her bridesmaids had 23. Norman Hartnell, who had outfitted her as bridesmaid to the Kents, produced a pearlwhite satin dress with a 15-foot train that fastened to the shoulders. It was embroidered with drop-pearls, seed-pearls and crystals, and had appliquéd orange-blossoms and star-flowers.

There were to be 2,000 guests. Although a number of these were official, a surprising percentage were not and – apart from relations (Philip's sisters were not asked, because they were all married to Germans and feelings were still raw so soon after the war) many were there through appreciation of services rendered.

They included the stationmaster from Wolferton, the stop for Sandringham, the schoolmistress from Birkhall, the riding-instructors from Elizabeth's childhood, the young women who had made her wedding dress, and an American lady who had sent parcels to Philip throughout the war. The event was to have film coverage with cameras positioned *outside* the Abbey. The service itself would be Broadcast on the radio.

Philip was also busy with preparations. He went to Lambeth Palace where, in a brief ceremony conducted by the Archbishop of Canterbury he converted from Greek orthodoxy to the Church of England. The groom had lost his Greek citizenship, and his title, when naturalised. He was now simply Lieutenant Philip Mountbatten, RN. Shortly before the wedding, however, the King made him Duke of Edinburgh and he was installed as a Knight of the Garter. His fiancée had received the Garter a week earlier.

The evening before the wedding he had a bachelor party at the Dorchester hosted by his uncle. He stayed the night at Kensington Palace and the next day left for the Abbey with the best man, David Milford Haven. If he suffered any pre-wedding jitters, he did not let them show. Nor did he have a cigarette, as he might normally have done. He had been a smoker, but had now promised his wife-to-be that he would give up as a wedding present.

RIGHT: Princess Elizabeth and Lieutenant Mountbatten pictured at Buckingham Palace in August 1947 following the announcement of their engagement.

The Archbishop of Canterbury officiated and the bride showed impeccable poise. Her father later wrote of escorting her to the altar: 'You were so calm and composed during the service & said your words with such conviction, that I knew everything was all right.'

While subsequent generations of royals have been able to honeymoon aboard the Royal Yacht *Britannia*, the princess and the duke instead went to Balmoral. When they returned to London the young couple occupied the same suite of rooms at Buckingham Palace that the princess had lived in when single and, by royal standards, this meant that they were somewhat cramped. They were supposed to reside at Clarence House in The Mall, but the building was so dilapidated that it required lengthy renovation. They did not move into Clarence House until the summer of 1949.

The King had given them Sunningdale Park near Windsor as a weekend country house. Before they could occupy it, however, the house was destroyed by fire. A replacement was quickly found in the shape of Windlesham Moor, a lavishly appointed house set in 50 acres of landscaped grounds not far from Ascot. While it promised them all the privacy they could hope for, it was ironic that Elizabeth faced the prospect of spending time there alone. Her husband, still a serving naval officer, was soon to be posted overseas.

In the meantime, their first child, Charles Philip Arthur George, was born in Buckingham Palace by Caesarean section 14 November 1948. The Princess was an indulgent mother and she had, at that stage in her life, time to devote to her son, but they would soon be separated.

In 1949 Philip was sent to Malta where his uncle, Lord Mountbatten, was commander of a cruiser squadron. The King was not happy about this posting for he knew Elizabeth would want to go too, and allowed her only on condition that she made regular returns to Britain. He needed his daughter to be able to deputise for him. A chain-smoker, he had developed lung cancer and he was finding it harder to meet the physical demands of his role.

LEFT: Official wedding portrait of the happy couple, 20 November 1947.

FOLLOWING PAGES: Scenes from the royal wedding, including (middle top) bridesmaids Princess Margaret and Princess Alexandra of Kent on their way to Westminster Abbey.

Charles stayed in London, the climate in Malta deemed unsuitable
for a young child of his years. The princess arrived in Valetta with 40
cases of clothing, her car and a polo pony. This game was a passion
among servicemen on the island and Philip, who had already proved
an extremely sound cricketer, was in the process of learning it.

The couple remained in Malta, on and off, between 1949 and
1951. Philip was given his own ship, HMS *Magpie*, which made a
number of leisurely official visits to Heads of State in the region.
Between calls there were cocktail parties, receptions, picnics and
swimming. Small wonder that *Magpie* was known in the Navy as
'Edinburgh's private yacht'.

Philip, despite his commitments, was inevitably drawn into public
life too. The couple had already made an official visit to Paris, and
now they were asked to undertake a tour of Canada and the USA
in October 1951. Such was the worry about the King's health that
Elizabeth's Private Secretary carried with him a sealed envelope to
be opened in the event of his death. It contained an address to both
houses of Parliament.

They spent a month in Canada and the USA. where they
stayed at Blair House (the White House was being renovated) as
guests of the Trumans. The President was very taken with them,
sending the King a message afterwards that: 'They went to the
hearts of all the citizens. As one father to another,' he went on,
'you can be very proud.'

Having proved themselves both officially and personally, they were
asked by the government to perform the same duty the following
year. This time it would be a much longer tour, lasting six months in
all, to Australia and New Zealand, visiting Kenya and Ceylon on the
way. Philip was given indefinite leave from the Navy. His full-time job
-- at least until his father-in-law's health improved – was to support his
wife in her official duties.

On 31 January 1952 they departed from Britain by air and the
King, Queen and Margaret saw them off. Although pictures of this

RIGHT: The King and
Queen with Princess
Margaret at London
Airport to say goodbye to
Princess Elizabeth and the
Duke of Edinburgh as they
left for their Australian
tour. This was the last
picture *The Daily Mail*
photographers ever took of
the King.

event show the King looking stooped and unwell, his family were optimistic. The tour would be extremely taxing, so it was arranged that in Kenya she and Philip would have, after a few days of official functions, a rest amid the idyllic scenery of the highlands.

They stayed at Saguna Lodge, their wedding present from the colony, and on 5 February 1952 they arrived at the Treetops Hotel. Built into a giant wild fig tree, the structure was not a conventional hotel but a series of private rooms and a viewing platform in the branches above a watering-hole.

Far away, at Sandringham, the Royal family retired to bed. The King had spent a highly enjoyable day's shooting, but during the night he died of thrombosis. The news did not reach his daughter through the intended official channels. The codename for this event – planned, like everything to do with royalty, long in advance – was 'Hyde Park Corner'. The telegram did not get through because it is thought the operator mistook the contents for the address. The news was instead picked up by a journalist friend of Elizabeth's Private Secretary Martin Charteris, passed by him to the duke's Equerry Michael Parker and thence to Philip and to Elizabeth. She flew home by the most direct route across North Africa.

Driven to St James's Palace, she made an accession speech that was brief and poignant: 'My heart is too full for me to say more to you today than that I shall always work as my father did.' Shortly afterwards she went on to Sandringham where her father lay in state in the church. She curtsied to his coffin – the last time she would ever make such a gesture.

LEFT: The funeral procession of King George VI at Windsor, 15 February 1952.

THE YOUNG QUEEN

For the second time in her life, Elizabeth had to move to Buckingham Palace from a home she loved. This time she gave up Clarence House more or less at the moment she and Philip had finished turning it into a family home.

Despite the training she had had, there remained much to learn about the day-to-day work of being monarch. She was later to recall that, thrust into her position: 'It was all very sudden, kind of taking on and making the best job you can . . . a question of just maturing into what you're doing and accepting that here you are and it's your fate.'

At least her coronation was not one of her principal worries. It would take place in June 1953 – 16 months after her accession – to allow time for the preparations to be organised.

As early as the previous November the route was timed and tested. In December the Abbey was closed for a period of nine months and handed over to the Ministry of Works, which began the task of transforming it for the ceremony. All the chairs were removed and rows of benches were constructed, as steeply raked as the seats in a theatre. Once complete they were crowded with soldiers to test their strength. Balconies were decorated with blue-and-gold hangings. In the crossing, which for crownings is known as the Theatre, the Coronation Chair was set. Behind it was the dais, five steps high (so that the sovereign could be clearly seen) and copied from a medieval original, on which she would sit to receive the homage of her noblemen.

The Queen listened to records made of her father's coronation ceremony, memorising the order of prayers and hymns and movements. Draped in sheets to help her become accustomed to carrying a long train, she processed around the White Drawing Room, while in the Picture Gallery, chairs were arranged into an approximation of the state coach so that she could practise embarking and disembarking.

There was, however, a dark cloud overshadowing the event. The new Queen's grandmother was in rapidly failing health and her death would oblige the court to go into mourning. The older Queen had suffered several major blows since the death of her husband in 1936: the

PREVIOUS SPREAD: The Queen returns to Buckingham Palace after her coronation, 2 June 1953.

TOP: The Queen, the Duke of Edinburgh and their children enjoy a family picnic and photo shoot, 1951.

BOTTOM RIGHT: The Queen and the Duke of Edinburgh at Balmoral with Prince Charles and Princess Anne.

BOTTOM LEFT: Again at Balmoral in the summer of 1952.

abdication; the war; the death of her son, George, in 1942; and the death of her son, the King, at the age of only 56. The single thing she hoped to see was her granddaughter wearing the crown. When the date was set for June, it became a race against time that she knew she would lose but she would not allow her own situation to interfere with the sovereign's crowning, insisting that court mourning should not be imposed if she died beforehand. She died on 24 March. It is believed that Elizabeth visited her before she passed away – and put on the crown.

For spectators who could not get to London, the ceremony was to be televised. It was initially announced that there would be no cameras in the Abbey. The result was such an outcry that the issue had to be reconsidered. The Government, the Church and the Queen were all opposed, as it was a formal religious service, and it was thought that the presence of camera crews would detract from the solemnity of the occasion. The service was also to last for seven hours and 15 minutes. Could an audience, even seated comfortably at home, endure such a marathon? The final decision was left to the Queen and ultimately she agreed to part of the ceremony being televised.

It was the Queen who decided to extend the route that would be followed by her carriage through London after the coronation, so that more people would have the chance to see her. She also asked that places along the way be especially allocated to schoolchildren. In the days before 2 June, London filled with visitors and participants, the latter including some 15,000 troops who would line the streets or march in the procession. Their tents filled the parks, which were made off-limits to civilians.

The day itself dawned misty, cold and very wet. At half past ten the State Coach emerged from the palace gates. The thousands who lined The Mall (around two million well-wishers were to crowd the streets that day) erupted in a tidal wave of cheering. Preceded by the Sovereign's Escort of Household Cavalry, the Queen and her consort moved down The Mall at walking pace (the coach is too heavy to travel any faster). The

RIGHT: The Duke of Edinburgh poses with the newly-crowned Queen in the throne room at Buckingham Palace.

coach turned down Whitehall and traversed Parliament Square to arrive at the Abbey's West Door.

Waiting inside was a congregation of more than 8,000 that included the prime ministers of the Commonwealth countries. The service – all seven hours of it – was watched on three million televisions in Britain by up to 27 million viewers, four-fifths of the population. Many people bought the first television their family had owned in order to see the ceremony.

International live broadcasts were not possible at that time, but the ceremony could be heard live on the radio overseas and later watched at the cinema as a film narrated by actress Anna Neagle.

The queen had arrived wearing an elaborately embroidered dress but she re-appeared, as custom dictated, in a 'linen shift' in order to present an image of simplicity and humility. On top of this, as the ceremony went on, was placed her long, velvet-and-ermine robe, embroidered in gold by a team at the Royal School of Needlework. She was then given the accoutrements of office: the orb, the sceptre and the amulets (a gift from the Commonwealth). Last came the St Edward's Crown, a replacement dating from the Coronation of Charles II for the original that had disappeared at the time of Cromwell. It weighed seven pounds – in addition to the 17 pounds of her robes.

The crown symbolises the history of the nation and Empire. One of its stones – a sapphire – is reputed to have belonged to the Abbey's first builder, Edward the Confessor. Another was owned by Mary, Queen of Scots. Another – the Black Prince's Ruby – was actually worn by King Henry V at Agincourt and again by Richard III at Bosworth. A fourth was worn in exile by King James II. The crown even incorporates the pearl earrings of Elizabeth I.

Philip, also in ermine-lined velvet robes, was the first secular figure to pay her homage. Her mother and sister were both present, watching from a gallery nearby. Her son, not yet five, was there, too, although he had not been considered old enough to watch the entire ceremony and

LEFT: The Queen poses for an official portrait against a backdrop at Buckingham Palace following her coronation.

had been spirited in only for the most important phase. Her daughter, less than three, was altogether too young and had been left at home, where there was a children's party going on.

It might have come as a pleasant surprise to those who regretted the fact that Britain, with her swiftly contracting empire, had been replaced by America as the western world's leading superpower, that at least 40,000 Americans came to London for the coronation and that berths aboard the Atlantic liners were all but impossible to obtain. In addition to these, an estimated 55 million – almost a third of the population – watched the ceremony on television in the USA, the Royal Air Force flying over the BBC tapes so that it could be screened within hours.

Once the coronation was over, the next event was a tour of the Commonwealth. It would last six months, from 25 November 1953 to 15 May 1954 and the Queen's children would not see their parents for all that time. Although she set off aboard the SS *Gothic* the Queen was to travel the final stretch from Malta aboard the Royal Yacht. Planned and begun before King George's death, the ship had been completed after Elizabeth's accession, and was launched by her. She decided to discontinue the name *Victoria and Albert* (there had been three of these), instead choosing *Britannia*.

At 412 feet in length and weighing 5,862 tons, the yacht was the size of a small warship and as luxurious as a country house. The yacht had a State Dining Room that could seat 56 (and doubled as a cinema), as well as a drawing room, separate sitting rooms for the Queen and the Duke, accommodation for the Household, their staff and the crew, and a 'barracks' for the Marine band that accompanied them on official visits.

At home, there was a simmering problem. Princess Margaret become involved in a relationship that was considered unsuitable. Group Captain Peter Townsend had been an equerry of her father's. He was a Battle of Britain fighter pilot, and King George had wanted one of these men attached to his staff as a tribute to their courage. Townsend was a success with the family. He was charming, modest, efficient, and had a pleasant sense of humour. There might have been no strenuous objection

TOP: Prime Minister Winston Churchill joined *Britannia* for the final leg of the Commonwealth Tour as the ship brought the Queen safely home up the Thames.

BOTTOM: The Queen drives Prince Charles and Princess Anne in her car at Windsor, 1957.

to the Queen's sister marrying this presentable commoner, but for the fact that Townsend was divorced. The Anglican Church, of which the Queen was head, could not sanction such a high-profile union involving a divorcee. The matter was kept from press and public until a journalist spotted Margaret outside the abbey following the coronation, make some adjustment to the uniform of an RAF officer, who was soon identified. It was a gesture of such obvious intimacy that the game was up.

Public opinion supported Margaret's right to marry the man she loved, yet if she did so she would have to give up all the privileges of her rank. Both parties discussed the future and decided that it was not viable for them to remain together.

The coronation had awakened a sense of pageantry as well as patriotism, and the Royal Family was able once again to provide a focus for this. The Queen attended Trooping the Colour dressed not – as she had been in the 1940s – in a dark blue uniform with a peaked cap, but in a magnificent scarlet cutaway coat in the pattern of the 18th century and faced with the buttons of whichever regiment was parading its colour that day. She wore a dark blue long skirt and a low, black hat of unique design on which the regiment's cap-badge and plume were displayed. She sat side-saddle, a thing she never did when riding for pleasure but which gave her an appropriate dignity. When going to and from this event along The Mall, she looked straight ahead and remained expressionless, a soldier on duty, attending a parade concentrating with appropriate seriousness.

Despite an affectionate marriage, the Queen and Prince Philip were often apart, especially in 1956 when he went, with his wife's blessing, on a voyage on *Britannia* that lasted four months. After opening the Melbourne Olympics, he visited a number of British territories that, because of their isolation, did not see Royalty from one reign to the next: the Falkland Islands, Tristan da Cuhna, St Helena. This meant, of course, that he was away from his growing children and missed Christmas with them.

The Queen and Philip eventually met in Portugal on a state visit. Apparently, knowing that Philip had grown a beard at one point during the his voyage, when he was reunited with his wife aboard an aircraft she,

TOP LEFT: In the 1950s, the Queen adopted more colourful uniforms for Trooping the Colour than she had done in previous years.

TOP RIGHT: The Queen makes her Christmas television broadcast from Sandringham, 1957.

BOTTOM: Prince Charles and Princess Anne paddling in rock pools in Malta with Lord and Lady Mountbatten, 1954.

and her ladies-in-waiting, were all sporting false whiskers.

Amid the stresses of her new role, the Queen found enormous pleasure in escaping to the world of the turf. In 1949 she and her mother, who had a similar wish to dabble in racing, had been persuaded to purchase a steeplechaser called Monaveen. Sadly, Monaveen died during a race and, while her mother remained devoted to steeplechasing, the then Princess Elizabeth decided to abandon 'the sticks' for flat racing. Only after the death of the Queen Mother in 2002 would her daughter take over her 'jumpers'.

The Queen regularly attended race meetings and, since her husband did not share her enthusiasm, she was often in the company of Henry Herbert, Lord Porchester. She had known him since they were both at Windsor during the war, and in 1969 she would appoint him her Racing Manager. They spoke frequently on the phone and his calls were put through immediately by the Palace switchboard. Given a thoroughbred as a wedding present, the Queen had begun a lifelong career as breeder and owner. The Royal Stud was moved to Sandringham from Hampton Court and blossomed under her patronage.

The Queen retained a great deal of her father's style in the way she reigned. There were no immediate alterations, although the monarchy became – in small ways – more informal during the 1950s. A small but characteristic change was that palace footmen no longer wore in their hair a white 'powder' concocted from flour and water, stiffened with soap and starch. The Queen, always considerate towards her servants, no doubt won their gratitude when she put a stop to it in 1955.

It was announced in 1957 that the custom of presenting debutantes at court was to end the following year. Presentations were the major event of a young woman's 'coming out', something enjoyed, hated or viewed with impatience by the girls themselves, and cherished by their mothers. It had been said that Prince Philip, who attended the presentations, only smiled at the ugly ones. Presentations were replaced by an additional palace garden party, which was added to the two already held each summer.

There is another garden party, held in June, at Holyrood in

TOP: The Queen and Prince Philip, in the uniform of the Colonel-in-Chief of the Cameron Highlanders, as the regiment is presented with its new colours at Balmoral, 1955.

BOTTOM: The Queen and the Queen Mother became increasingly interested in horse racing during the 1950s.

Edinburgh, where the procedure is the same. Guests devour a tea (they consume 20,000 sandwiches) provided by Lyons, the caterers, and in the early years were offered strawberries and cream as well, although this was given up as too expensive.

Yet another change was the televising of the Christmas broadcast. These were begun, on wireless, by George V in 1932. His son had hated them and so did his granddaughter. The speeches were made live on the afternoon of Christmas Day, and understandably ruined the holiday for the sovereign, who could not relax until the job was done, although at least from 1960 it was possible to pre-record it.

The upbringing of the Queen's children was different to her own experience, and this too was an innovation. The Queen told palace staff that they need not bow and curtsy to her children until they were older, and need not address them as 'Royal Highness'. Their Christian names would be used instead. It was also a novelty that Prince Charles started school as an ordinary pupil, first at Hill House in Chelsea and then at his father's old prep school, Cheam. The press besieged the school with cameramen until the Queen summoned Fleet Street editors to ask them, in exchange for a single press opportunity at the school, to leave Charles in peace. The point of sending him to school had been, after all, to allow him to experience a normal education.

Another innovation of the decade was the advent of outright criticism of the monarch. Attacks in the press on the King or Queen had been commonplace in Hanoverian times, and had also been directed at the eldest son of Queen Victoria both before and after he became King. Queen Elizabeth was dutiful and conscientious enough not to merit strong criticism. Nevertheless, she had from the beginning of her reign courted rebuke by leaving her children for long periods while travelling abroad. It was also known that, on the night Prince Charles was rushed to Great Ormond Street Hospital for an emergency appendectomy, his mother had stayed at home in bed. This was mere sniper-fire in comparison with the broadsides that were to come in later years.

TOP: At Hill House School, Charles took part in a field gun drill similar to those normally seen at the Royal Tournament during his school field day, 1957.

BOTTOM: Prince Charles and his father take a boat ride at Cowes in the Isle of Wight, 1957.

Whatever a small minority of her subjects thought of her at home, the Queen had proved her value abroad, where Britain's relationship with her mightiest ally had come unstuck. The invasion of Egypt by French, British and Israeli troops to seize control of the Suez Canal in 1956 had proved a major humiliation. The operation had been cynical and ill-conceived, and America refused to support it. It was called off and the soldiers evacuated. The British public had considerably bruised feelings towards America. The USA felt that Britain had brought catastrophe on herself by embarking on such a rash adventure in the first place.

The following autumn, the Queen made a state visit to the USA – the 350th anniversary of the founding of Virginia made a handy excuse – to restore good relations. The visit was a greater success than anyone could have predicted. It was the Americans' first chance to see the young Queen, and they were charmed – as others had been – by her combination of personal shyness and official gravity.

She was given a ticker-tape parade in New York, and greeted by a huge turnout in Washington. No modern American president has yet declined to be seen with British Royalty, and Eisenhower was in any case an old wartime acquaintance. Delighted by this reception, she was willing to set aside a certain amount of formality. The press at home noticed that she had been at close quarters – almost mingling – with crowds and one paper, the *Daily Herald*, asked: 'People here have been reading of the Queen going about freely among ordinary people, behaving like an ordinary person. Canada loved it. America was bowled over by it. Why is it not allowed to happen here?'

Seeing the enthusiasm of crowds that greeted her, an American commentator observed: 'There goes Britain's ultimate diplomatic weapon.' She had saved Anglo-American relations during a very sticky patch, refocusing attention on the two countries' shared heritage instead of their divergent world-views.

As well as being instrumental in sealing good relations with the West's great superpower, the queen was also deployed in the Cold War against the Communist world. Her visit to Ghana soon after its independence in

RIGHT: Prince Charles attending Cheam School in Berkshire, 1958.

1957 was both a personal and a symbolic triumph, helping to turn opinion among regional rulers away from Moscow. The Soviet Union saw Africa as an important ideological battleground, and was able to throw around a good deal of Marxist rhetoric that resonated with the peoples there. Ghana was unstable and ruled by a president, Kwame Nkrumah, whose autocratic style had made him unpopular. He was sufficiently unpopular, in fact, to be the likely target of assassination, and thus put at risk anyone in his company. He had become a tireless – even meddling – champion of anti-imperialism, and was loud in his condemnation of the colonial power that the Queen personified, so Her Majesty might well have expected an awkward meeting.

Despite these factors she went ahead with the visit, and Nkrumah was delighted. Her appearance with him added to his standing with his people, increasing perception of him as an international statesman. Britain had just given independence to Ghana – hardly the act of an oppressor – and the fact that its ruler visited in person made a very positive impression on the people. They crowded to look at her at every opportunity and, when she discovered that they were disappointed not to see her wearing more jewellery, she obliged by putting on in public every stone she had available. One could not imagine Khrushchev being able to compete with that!

LEFT: The Queen addresses the General Assembly of the United Nations in New York, 21 October 1957.

CHAPTER FIVE: 1960–1970

❧

A GROWING FAMILY

By the beginning of the 1960s the Queen had, as she had put it, 'matured into' her office. Her apprenticeship was long over, with her family growing up and her two children starting on their own life's-journeys. Her habits were well established, the year divided between London, Windsor, Norfolk, Edinburgh and Aberdeenshire. She and Philip were on the verge of middle life and, as he put it: 'I would have thought that we're entering the least interesting period of our kind of glamorous existence.'

Public opinion seemed to agree, and viewing figures for the Christmas broadcast were declining. Far from fading into obscurity, the Queen aroused widespread interest by having two more children, Andrew (1960) and Edward (1964). The media did not, however, have a field day over these new arrivals. Her Majesty decided that this second pair of Royal children should have greater privacy than their older siblings had enjoyed. Press access to them was restricted and Prince Andrew was not even seen by the public until a month after he was born, fuelling rumours that he was in some way abnormal.

Another event early in the decade that generated an upsurge of public interest was the marriage of Princess Margaret, who had found happiness with a photographer, Antony Armstrong-Jones, and married him at Westminster Abbey in February 1960.

Her friendship and subsequent marriage to 'Tony' – who had taken portraits of the Royals – was initially very happy and brought the monarchy into the same social orbit as the likes of Peter Sellers and Mick Jagger. This connection was not universally welcome. Prince Philip (the Queen had by now made him a British Prince) and his new brother-in-law were entirely incompatible personalities, and courtiers regarded him – despite his Eton and Cambridge background – as a tradesman.

The tabloid media had by now got into its stride, and the behaviour of the family was examined more closely. With their frequent travels and the children's schooling, there was plenty to write about, and newspaper readers became increasingly judgemental about the Royals.

PREVIOUS SPREAD: The Queen, Prince Charles, Princess Margaret and Prince Andrew en route to Sandringham for Christmas, 1962.

LEFT: The baby Prince Andrew and Prince Charles disembarking from *Britannia*, 1960.

The sense of humour — or offhand rudeness, according to one's perspective — of the Queen's husband became so well-known that a book of his sayings — *The Wit of Prince Philip* — was published. Young, energetic, attractive and photogenic, the Royal Family had become a staple of the illustrated papers, much as the Kennedy family was in the United States.

The unprecedented press coverage of the Royal Family tended to make the public think of them as being just like any other family. In previous reigns, pictures of the family when off duty had shown them out shooting in Norfolk or the Highlands. Their tailored tweeds and Purdey shotguns were well beyond the financial reach of most of their subjects. Now the sovereign, her husband and children were pictured having picnics on Scottish beaches without a servant in sight, dressed in clothes that were old, comfortable and just like other peoples'. Increased prosperity amongst the general population meant that the visible differences between social classes had diminished and the public expected those in positions of privilege to be less remote. A poll found that three out of five people 'wanted the Royal Family to live more like ordinary people'.

Although they lived in the palace during the week, the Royal Family relaxed at weekends at Windsor. They had had one part of the castle — the Edward III Tower — renovated and made into a simple and modern dwelling. Hugh Casson designed the interiors, which were hung with paintings by artists such as Edward Seago and Sidney Nolan. The notion was that these premises would be self-catering, though in fact there were always staff in attendance. Although the press would love to have photographed it, this was and remains an entirely private domain despite being in the midst of a castle thronging with tourists.

The Queen had always seen Windsor as her home, Buckingham Palace as her office and the other residences as seasonal retreats. No other place evokes the same affection as Windsor — the oldest royal residence and the world's largest inhabited castle. Her Majesty not only enjoyed spending weekends there but decided, in 1964, that Christmas

TOP LEFT: Princess Margaret and Anthony Armstrong-Jones on the balcony at Buckingham Palace on their wedding day, 6 May 1960.

TOP RIGHT: Prince Andrew enjoying the summer weather at Balmoral with his mother, 1962.

BOTTOM RIGHT: The Queen Mother with Prince Charles, Princess Anne and Prince Andrew on her 60th birthday, 4 August 1960.

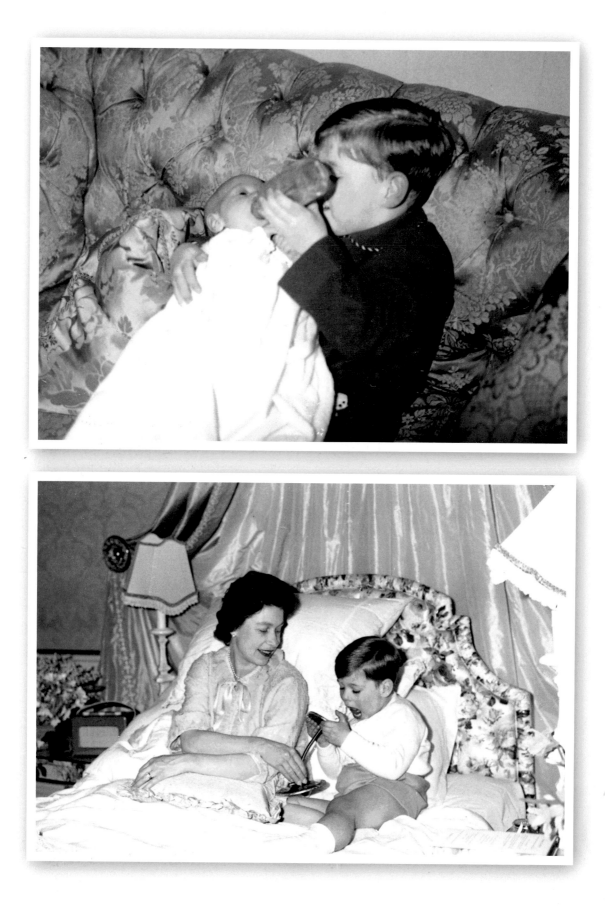

would be celebrated there instead of at Sandringham. This practice was to last until 1988, when the family returned to Norfolk for the duration of the festive season.

Christmas among the royals is a major event that begins with the taping of the Queen's broadcast. Until 1957 this was a live radio broadcast, then was live on television until 1960, at which time it became possible to pre-record. This not only avoided ruining Her Majesty's Christmas Day but also meant that the film could be sent to Commonwealth countries in time for 25 December. The broadcasts, always played at 3.00 p.m., are watched in the royal household, too. The programmes take the form of a survey of the previous 12 months, and enable the Queen to give personal reactions to events. Although the thoughts are her own, her delivery is still formal for she is reciting prepared remarks. When once asked to be more spontaneous, she retorted: 'I'm not an actress!'

The entire family gathers for Christmas, including the Kents, Gloucesters and Ogilvys. Gifts are opened on Christmas Eve, a reflection of the Family's Germanic past, Prince Albert having introduced many of their particular customs. The tree comes from the Sandringham Estate and the decorations, as in many families, are heirlooms.

On the day itself the morning is devoted to church. All the royals are present as the media is there in force and the image of Royal Family, united in worship, is important. A lengthy lunch follows, but must be finished before three o'clock, when the family watches the Queen's address in respectful silence. The evening is spent enjoying party games, the most popular of which is charades. It is well known that the Queen excels at this. Despite her outburst that 'I am not an actress!' she apparently does have considerable talent for doing impressions of prime ministers and world leaders she has met.

The Queen had, apparently, always wanted four children. The first two had been born before she came to the throne, but after she had become a reigning monarch there was simply no time for others. The

TOP: Prince Andrew helping to feed his younger brother, Prince Edward, 1964.

BOTTOM: Prince Andrew pulls faces in his mother's vanity mirror at Buckingham Palace following the birth of his baby brother Edward, 10 March 1964.

fact that she was able to resume motherhood in the 1960s was another sign that she had settled into her role. The experience of the younger pair was to be different to that of their siblings. Neither was to be treated with the same rigour that Charles experienced.

This did not, however, mean either mountains of toys or a licence to misbehave. All four children were brought up in the care of strict nursery staff and under the equally stern eye of their parents. All of them learned that their behaviour mattered because they were so much in the public eye. Their father taught them to be punctiliously polite, not least to servants, and they were sent to apologise if they were ever found to have been rude.

The Queen deferred to her husband in the matter of their children's upbringing. He was head of the family, and she wished him to make the decisions that involved their private life. The fact that he could be tough, impatient and demanding was, she felt, necessary. She shared his view, for instance, that Charles was too sensitive, making no attempt to protect him from Philip's often loud disapproval.

It could be said that the Queen was a distant parent, but distant does not mean unaffectionate, and she was highly attentive within the limits her official life allowed. She greatly enjoyed motherhood. She devoted time to her children every day (she and Philip always bathed them in the evenings), and she put back by half an hour her weekly Tuesday evening audience with the Prime Minister because it clashed with their bedtime. She could not, however, afford to make them the highest priority in her life. She was far busier than any normal working mother, and it was a matter of duty with her that her job always came first. This attitude was bred into her and explains how she could undertake a six-month Commonwealth tour while her first children were still small. Whatever her personal feelings, she could not let millions down by failing in her duty.

A thoughtful, sensitive and often timid child, Charles was by now an adolescent, and was in many ways the antithesis of his father, who had sought to instil in him a toughness that was not in his nature.

TOP LEFT: Prince Philip ready for a swim on holiday in the Mediterranean, 1964.

TOP RIGHT: The Royal Family photographed on the Queen's 39th birthday, 1965.

BOTTOM: The Queen with Prince Andrew and Princess Ann at Balmoral, 1964.

Charles's response had been to draw closer to his grandmother. The Queen Mother saw in him a shyness reminiscent of her husband. In 1962 he went to school at Gordonstoun. Although he knew something of it through his father, the culture shock was considerable. A non-academic school whose objective was character-building rather than exam passes, the isolation of its Highland setting was matched by a Spartan lifestyle that emphasised adventure training and self-reliance. It had suited Philip extremely well, developing his qualities of leadership, but it was entirely the wrong place for a boy of Charles's nature.

His father had thought it would toughen him up, but instead it drove him further into his shell. Instead of being befriended by the socially ambitious, the opposite happened – he was shunned by boys who feared accusations of toadying. He was deeply unhappy, and reluctant to return at the beginning of each term. Even though he had some eventual success at school, becoming 'Keeper', or head boy, as his father had done, he left the school without regret and was to send his own sons elsewhere. By the time his brothers followed him to Gordonstoun, conditions had changed. Dormitories were no longer freezing, the regime was less hearty, and in Edward's time there were even girl pupils.

Unlike her brother, Anne had needed no grandmotherly support. She had inherited her uncomplicated, no-nonsense nature direct from Philip. She was sent to Benenden, a traditional girls' school in Kent. Confident and outgoing, she thrived in the sociable atmosphere, and became popular. With no academic ambitions, she developed instead what was to be her lifelong passion for riding and eventing. She honed her skills in this while at the school, and went on to combine them successfully with duties her position required.

The Queen's official life was relentlessly busy. Among her visitors were the Kennedys. Both the charismatic young President and his wife had previous connections with the Royal Family. His father had been American Ambassador just before the Second World War, and his mother and sisters had been presented at court. Mrs Kennedy,

LEFT: Rarely seen without her customary high heels, the Queen wore specially provided red sandals when visiting the tomb of Mahatma Gandhi in 1961.

formerly a photojournalist, had been sent to cover the coronation for American newspapers. The Kennedys were on the return journey to Washington from Paris, where Mrs Kennedy had received a tumultuous welcome and huge media attention. This adulation now spilled over to London, and the Kennedys were invited to dinner by the Queen, although Her Majesty was not impressed with the brash 'Hollywood' glamour that highlighted the Kennedys' style of statesmanship. Nevertheless when the terrible assassination in Dallas sent shock waves through the United Kingdom in 1963, the Queen gave permission for flags to be flown at half-mast across London, while her guardsmen wore black armbands on their uniforms. She was later to dedicate a permanent memorial – an acre of ground at Runnymede – to the president's memory and to share the occasion with his widow and children.

Britain underwent a significant change in 1964 when the Conservative Government was narrowly defeated in the general election and, for the first time since her accession, the Queen found herself dealing with a Labour Prime Minister. Harold Wilson was a decade older than the Queen, a Yorkshireman who made a virtue of his impoverished background. A former Oxford economics don, he had little in common with Her Majesty. Every one of the men who had previously attended weekly audiences with her – Churchill, Eden, Macmillan, Douglas-Home – had come from a hinterland of aristocracy and public school. Wilson was a new departure, yet both found the meetings a pleasure. Their genuine rapport was demonstrated by the fact that his audiences often overran the customary 20–30 minutes. He greatly enjoyed staying at Balmoral, and experiencing the informality and friendliness of the Queen. Accustomed to seeing her at audiences or state occasions, he was enchanted to find her cooking, washing dishes and driving herself about. Wilson undoubtedly loomed very large in her affections. In April 1976 she and Prince Philip were to attend his retirement dinner at Number Ten, a gesture she had not made for any Prime Minister but Churchill.

RIGHT: Prime Minister Harold Wilson and his wife, Mary, with The Queen and Prince Philip and the Prime Minister's retirement dinner in 10 Downing Street, 23 March 1976.

Throughout the 1960s the British Empire was being wound up throughout Africa and the West Indies. The alternative to British rule was not severance of all ties but the choice of maintaining cultural links, even in the case of a sovereign state, through membership of the Commonwealth (now called the Commonwealth of Nations rather than the British Commonwealth). There were distinct advantages, such as priority access to overseas aid from the United Kingdom, but there was also the kudos of contact with the Queen. She regularly attended the conference for Commonwealth Heads of Government. Images of them with royalty and with other leaders naturally enhanced their prestige at home. They were also able to 'network' among themselves.

The premiers of small countries met on equal terms with those of large, powerful ones. It was, as it still is, a statesman's club that attracts the envy of many outside. Were it not for the personal interest of the British monarch, it might well have met less regularly and died of neglect before it had had the chance to mature. In the decades that followed she would go further in her attachment: the conference would no longer be held invariably in Britain but in different venues throughout the world. No matter where it was, she and the duke would attend.

In May 1961, South Africa became a republic and was forced to leave the Commonwealth because of its racial policy. Its neighbour, Rhodesia, declared itself unilaterally independent four years later in order to maintain white minority rule. In Quebec, there were loud rumblings in favour of separation from the Canadian Federation and therefore from the Queen, who was to visit the province in 1964. It was stated in the press on both sides of the Atlantic that there was a plot to assassinate her and that this would be 'a second Dallas'. Her Majesty displayed the usual combination of courage and fatalism, letting it be known that: 'I am not worried about the visit. We are quite relaxed.' In the event, the huge security operation controlled potential troublemakers and the Queen encountered nothing more serious than a few displays of deliberate rudeness.

LEFT: The Royal Family at Frogmore, Windsor on the Queen's 42nd birthday in 1968.

At home, the British public continued to see — or wish to see — the Royals as a mirror image of themselves. The popular press had become steadily more intrusive, and the palace had realised that aloofness was not the answer when dealing with this. Better to accommodate them where possible, and maintain some influence over what they published. Public relations took a significant step forward when, in 1965, Australian William Heseltine was appointed Assistant Press Secretary. In the new climate of media relations that Heseltine built, the Queen granted permission for television networks to visit her homes. Two close advisors convinced her that the idea would be popular with the public. One was Lord Mountbatten, the other was his son-in-law, the film-maker Lord Brabourne. Mountbatten had just taken part in a series about his life that was shown on national television. It was widely watched, and he was very pleased with it. He felt that the royal homes of Britain would not only make interesting television but would give a hint of the life of the monarch in a way that would intrigue her subjects.

The series *Royal Palaces of Britain* was produced in 1966 by both television networks, BBC and ITV, together. This was a look at six residences, and was shown on Christmas Day that year. The programmes proved, as expected, immensely popular. It really created a sense of privilege that, as the publicity material announced: 'By kind permission of the Queen, cameras [are] allowed to enter into the private apartments of Britain's Royal Palaces for the first time.' The success of this venture soon gave birth to a bolder idea — a further documentary, this time not about the buildings but their inhabitants.

The result was not seen for a further three years. Simply titled *Royal Family*, although the press was to nickname it *Corgi and Beth*, the programme followed the Queen for a year in order to record the activities that were typical of her life and work. The family was seen cooking in the open air at Balmoral (Prince Philip, it transpired, had designed the barbecue equipment himself, and presided over it with his usual air of command). The Queen was also shown visiting a local shop to buy sweets for Prince Edward. The exchange of money, and

TOP: Princess Anne with Prince Andrew at the Badminton Horse Trials, April 1969.

BOTTOM RIGHT: Racing driver Graham Hill shows his Formula 1 car to Prince Charles, Lord Mountbatten and the Duke of Kent, July 1968.

BOTTOM LEFT: On his first day at Heatherdown Prep School in Ascot, Prince Andrew meets his headmaster, James Edwards, September 1968.

pleasantries, looked natural enough – although, of course, an entire camera crew had had to squeeze into the small premises, too. It was later claimed that, because the Queen carries no money, one of them had to lend her the cash.

The film took 75 days to shoot, and the result was vivid, informative and illuminating. Most who saw it were fascinated by these unprecedented glimpses of the private moments of such a public family. Once again, there was astonishment at how, when relaxing, they could seem so ordinary. Viewers were also impressed to see something of the mechanics of how the household was run, how hard the Queen worked and what she did all day.

The programme was shown twice – once by each network – during the month of June 1969, and was watched by two-thirds of all Britons. It was sold to 140 countries and earned £120,000 in profits, which were divided between the Queen and the broadcasters. Her Majesty donated her share to the Society of Film and Television Arts.

Royal Family greatly increased public interest in the monarchy. It also, however, set a new standard for intrusiveness. Having had such a detailed look at the private lives of the Queen and her family, the public was to regard such intimacy not as a privilege, but as a right. It is significant that the film has remained locked in the Royal Archives ever since. The Queen owns the copyright, and it cannot be shown without her express permission. Although excerpts are occasionally screened, the programme in its entirety has, for the present at least, vanished.

Less than two weeks after the screenings, public attention was again focused on royalty. Prince Charles, whom his mother had created Prince of Wales in 1958 when he was a schoolboy at Cheam, was now 21 and was to be formally invested as Prince at Caernarvon Castle. This event, the most important ceremony since the coronation, was an opportunity for Wales to stage a big state occasion. In charge of the arrangements was Antony Armstrong-Jones, who had been created Earl of Snowdon on his marriage to Princess Margaret. He had a flair for architectural design and established within the castle ruins

LEFT: Prince Edward flying high with Princess Anne and the Queen at Frogmore, Windsor, 1968.

a strikingly simple but grandiose setting. On the greensward – for the ceremony was entirely out of doors – was a plain circular dais of Welsh slate, accommodating three thrones, also of Welsh slate, for the Prince and his parents. A swooping canopy provided protection from the elements but, because the ceremony had to be visible to television cameras at different angles, this was made of transparent Perspex, held up by what looked like giant spears.

Striking and very contemporary, the design looked like the stage set for a Shakespeare play, and was, in fact, created by a theatrical designer. A simple and very modern gold chaplet was made for the prince – again, this looked rather like a stage prop – and he wore the uniform of the recently established Royal Regiment of Wales.

The ceremony itself was somewhat contrived. For centuries, Princes of Wales had been connected to the principality in name only. They had assumed their title in London or Windsor without any formalities. Only in 1911, when George V's eldest son (the Duke of Windsor) had been invested had the Welsh Cabinet Minister, Lloyd George, suggested making a public spectacle of it. In 1969, as in 1911, most Welsh were delighted, but this time there was resentment from a noisy element of nationalists, the Free Wales Army, which threatened to disrupt what they saw as the celebration of an alien dynasty's presence in their country. There were bomb threats and even explosions – one device blew off a boy's leg, another killed the man who was setting it. Security was tight as the royals, government officials and the public descended on Caernarvon, but the weather held, the crowds were enthusiastic, the extremists did no damage that day, and 1 July 1969 entered history.

Later that year Prince Philip triggered something of a crisis when interviewed on television in America. He dropped the bombshell of announcing that the following year the Royal Family would go 'into the red', for the Queen's Civil list allowance of £475,000 a year had not been increased since she came to the throne. He was to follow this by remarking that: 'We may have to move into a smaller home.'

TOP: Prince Charles, accompanied by the Queen Mother, is installed as a Knight of the Garter at Windsor Castle, 1968.

BOTTOM: The Perspex canopy covering the ceremonial area for the investiture of Prince Charles.

CHAPTER SIX: 1970–1980

SILVER JUBILEE

In many ways this was a decade best forgotten. For the first time, large-scale terrorism became a feature of British life when the Ulster troubles, dormant for a generation, re-surfaced. Troops backed up the police in keeping order as gunshots and explosions became a routine night time sound in Belfast and Londonderry. Kidnappings and assassinations became so commonplace as to merit only brief media interest. Judges, policemen and anyone linked with the British Government was at daily risk.

Elsewhere in the country, industrial relations were to reach their worst level since the Depression. Strikes and shortages were frequent and many people's memories of the 1970s are of power cuts, militant strikers and rampant inflation. Images of families dining at home by candlelight at the time of the three-day week were soon joined by the grimy look of the Punk movement, a deliberate and anarchic ugliness that suited Britain's status as what people in other countries referred to as the 'Sick Man of Europe.'

The Royal Family was, naturally, not immune to conditions in the country. Their position at the pinnacle of the British establishment made them a prime target for terrorists. The Royals were not difficult to track, since their movements were listed each day in the Court Circular, and specific events were often announced long months in advance. They did not hide, and were frequently in front of crowds that would give cover to an attacker.

When riding on horseback to and from Horse Guards for the Trooping the Colour, the Queen could hardly have been more conspicuous – seated above the heads of the crowd and moving at walking pace. No American president would dream of being so exposed in public, yet the Queen would countenance no compromise. The Royals were a security nightmare but once again the quiet, dogged courage with which the Queen and her family continued their routine of visits and speeches and ceremonies was resoundingly impressive and reassuring. 'So long as she's carrying on as usual,' people seemed to feel, 'things can't be that bad.'

PREVIOUS SPREAD: The Queen and Prince Philip wave to the crowds from the balcony at Buckingham Palace during the Silver Jubilee celebrations, 7 June 1977.

LEFT: The Queen acknowledges the cheers of the crowds during her 1970 visit to New Zealand.

To add the security headaches, 1970 became the year of the first 'walkabout', a custom that permanently changed the way in which the monarchy was seen by the public, and which the Queen saw as the beginning of a new relationship with her subjects. The term was associated with Australian aborigines, describing a period spent wandering in the Bush. To the sovereign, and her family, it meant travelling short distances on foot, stopping to talk to well-wishers.

The first walkabout took place in Wellington, New Zealand, in March that year, though the Maltese claim that the Queen made precisely the same sort of informal progress in the streets of Valetta during a visit three years earlier. In Wellington, the Queen and Prince Philip, with Charles and Anne, were due to attend a function at the Town Hall. They arrived by car, but instead of being driven to the entrance, leaving onlookers with no more than a glimpse of waving glove, they disembarked in the square outside and walked all the way round the building to its front door. In the process, thousands of people saw or photographed them, many also shaking hands or speaking to them. This was no more a spontaneous event than anything the Queen does when on duty. It had been suggested, and planned, by the city authorities as a way of involving local people more closely in the event.

The second walkabout took place a few months later in Coventry, and was also a huge success, setting a pattern that has been followed ever since. It makes life extremely difficult for security staff to have the Queen moving slowly through crowds and pausing all the time. That she has remained safe is a tribute to those who look after her. During walkabouts the Queen often accepts bouquets from numerous well-wishers. After holding one for a few minutes she will discreetly pass it on to those who accompany her, and bystanders become used to the sight of a man in a suit juggling bunches of flowers. There are always at least four people following the Queen – her Private Secretary, her Equerry, her protection officer and a lady-in-waiting.

TOP LEFT: A pensive Prince Edward on his first day at Gibbs pre-prep school in Kensington, September 1971.

TOP RIGHT: The Queen's first British 'walkabout' in Coventry, June 1970.

BOTTOM: Prime Minister Edward Heath plays host to the Queen and President Richard Nixon at Chequers while Mrs Nixon sniffs the roses, October 1970.

Well aware of the trouble people often take to see her, the Queen will make herself as visible as she can. Her appearance is always similar. Although the cut and colour of her outfits will vary, the basic elements remain constant. The most important point is that she should be conspicuous. She must stand out in a crowd so that those who have come to see her will not be disappointed. This is why she wears suits and dresses and hats of a uniform colour, often a pastel shade such as pink or pale yellow or orange. It was Queen Mary who began this practice of dressing in pastels, making the Queen the third generation to do so. On occasions when she has been with other royal ladies – her mother, sister or daughter – each of them would be dressed in a different colour so that distant crowds could distinguish them.

The shade of her costume may well, of course, be chosen to reflect her circumstances. If she is visiting the Irish Guards, something she wears will be in 'St Patrick's blue', the colour of their regimental hackle. The Queen is always formally dressed in public. She wears accoutrements – a hat and gloves – that by the 1970s were rarely still seen on ladies. Those she meets on official visits will be dressed up, and she cannot look less elegant than they do. She always wears gloves because she must shake hands with dozens if not scores of people at a time, and the gloves are often white so that her waving hand will be visible to distant onlookers. To avoid bruising on these occasions, her handshake is deliberately limp and she keeps her little finger out of the way. For this reason, too, she wears no rings on her right hand. On her left she has only her wedding and engagement rings, and her gold-and-platinum watch, a gift from France, is always worn outside her glove on her left wrist.

The Queen's skirts are carefully tailored to ensure that they never blow in the wind, and must allow for the fact that she is often seated on platforms above others. Her hats do not have brims so wide as to hide her face, and must not be so flimsy that a gust of wind will carry them off. The style she favoured during the 1960s

TOP: The Queen Mother at Badminton Horse Trials in 1970 with Prince Andrew, Viscount Linley and other royal youngsters enjoying ice lollies.

MIDDLE LEFT: Princes Andrew and Philip at Gordonstoun School on the 13-year-old prince's first day, September 1973.

MIDDLE RIGHT: Prince Philip and the Queen with the Duchess of Windsor outside her Paris home, May 1972.

BOTTOM LEFT: A family portrait at Buckingham Palace for the Silver Wedding of the Queen and Prince Philip, 1972.

BOTTOM RIGHT: The Queen and Prince Philip admiring Highland cattle at Balmoral, 1972.

and 1970s was the kind of head-hugging 'helmet' shape that could be put on and forgotten. In later decades she would conspicuously favour brimmed hats with high, flat crowns, and these also help to make her noticeable.

Her Majesty's hairstyle is the result of careful planning. Until the 1960s she had a side parting and a looser, more girlish look. By the time she reached her forties she had the swept-up, tight and tidy arrangement she has retained ever since. Inconspicuous, yet familiar to the public from her portraits on banknotes, this is such a part of a national image that to change it would seem almost like redesigning the flag. Her shoes are high-heeled for additional height, although they must be suitable for the vast amount of standing she is obliged to do. Even her posture is a matter not of natural inclination but of forethought and training. The Queen adopts a standing posture with her feet slightly apart and her weight equally balanced, remaining thus for hours without drooping, looking tired or otherwise showing the strain she must feel.

Everything that the Queen wears is the result of meticulous preparation far in advance. Even if she is receiving for 20 minutes the commanding officer of an army unit, she will have on a brooch with the regimental crest – and may then replace it with something else for her next audience. For a typical visit – and in any year there are about 30 trips to various parts of Britain – planning starts months ahead and every item is chosen, made or cleaned. For the Queen's Silver Jubilee in 1977, deciding on the dresses she would wear for the tours and other celebrations began in 1975.

The wardrobe chosen by the Queen in private life is, by contrast to her official 'uniform', that of any genteel farmer's wife – tweed and wool skirts, cotton day-dresses, headscarves, clothes for walking and handling dogs. Her garments are invariably more practical, more comfortable, and often off-the-peg, though they will always be altered to ensure a perfect fit. She choses to wear Daks skirts, and Burberry and Barbour coats.

TOP: The Queen receives a golden sword from His Highness Sheikh Isa bin Sulman al Khalifa, Emir of Bahrain, during her 1972 visit.

BOTTOM: The Royal Family at Westminster Abbey during the Thanksgiving Service for the Queen and Prince Philip's Silver Wedding, November 1972.

The Queen relaxes in the manner she prefers — *The Daily Telegraph* crossword, walking the dogs, assembling jigsaws and watching television. In the 1970s she, and her mother, enjoyed *Dad's Army* with its innocent humour and wartime camaraderie. She also regularly watched the 1975 historical epic *Edward VII*. Naturally, she had a close interest in the subject, and was disappointed whenever she missed an episode. This was, of course, before the availability of video recorders, but within days the BBC would send her the necessary film reels so that she could catch up.

The 1970s were years of high visibility for the Royals, whose family celebrations offered some of the decade's few bright moments. The Queen and Prince Philip marked their Silver Wedding anniversary with a thanksgiving service in November 1972. Almost exactly a year later, in Westminster Abbey on 14 November 1973, Princess Anne became the first of their children to marry when she and cavalry officer Captain Mark Phillips became husband and wife. Visits, both domestic and overseas, by the Queen and her relations reached a crescendo at the time of her Silver Jubilee in 1977, and in the same year, she became a grandmother when Princess Anne's first child, Peter, was born.

In March 1974 there was an attempt to kidnap Princess Anne. As she was being driven along The Mall returning from an engagement one evening with her husband, a lady-in-waiting, a police protection officer and a chauffeur, another vehicle suddenly screeched out of a side road and blocked their way. An armed man leapt out and ran toward them. Jim Beaton, their protection officer, jumped out and put himself in front of the Princess. His own weapon jammed and the gunman, Ian Ball, shot him three times. The chauffeur attempted to disarm Ball and was also shot. A passing journalist, Brian McConnell, then tackled Ball and was shot in the chest before a member of the public, Ron Russell, punched Ball to the ground. A police officer who came across the kidnapping was also shot before Ball was finally overpowered when more police arrived. Ian Ball was

TOP: The Queen steps ashore from Britannia in the Maldives on her Far East tour, 1972.

BOTTOM: The Queen and Prince Philip walking their dogs with Princes Andrew and Edward at Balmoral, September 1972.

an unbalanced personality who had become obsessed with mounting this operation. He had planned for three years to kidnap the princess and hold her to ransom for three million pounds.

All of those who had been injured recovered from their wounds. Beaton was awarded the George Cross. Hills and Russell were awarded the George Medal while the chauffeur, Alex Callander, along with McConnell and the police officer who gave chase to and arrested Ball, Peter Edmonds, were awarded the Queen's Gallantry Medal. This had been an anxious moment for all concerned, and led to an extensive review of security arrangements.

The Royal Family came in for an increasing amount of criticism during the 1970s on the grounds that they were too expensive. Prince Philip's remarks in America a few years earlier had caused horror and embarrassment at home, where many were now suffering serious financial hardship. It seemed both insensitive and insulting that such a wealthy family should cast itself as somehow deprived. There was public outcry over the Royal Family's income from Civil List funding, resulting in not one, but two Parliamentary Enquiries into the subject, in 1971 and 1975. The first took place under Edward Heath's Conservative Government, the second under a Labour administration led by Harold Wilson. Neither man and neither party had any desire to embarrass the monarch, but the Civil List income had to be brought into the light of day and investigated. One emotional issue was that of income tax, which the Queen did not pay. This situation was not a matter of course. Although George V and VI had not paid tax, Edward VII and Victoria had. The Queen's exemption seemed an insult to her cash-strapped people, but both Heath and Wilson decided to continue this status. Parliament also concluded both enquiries by voting a substantial increase in the Civil List. Prince Philip's forthrightness had won the day.

These increases, naturally, added fuel to the flames for those who thought the monarchy an expensive luxury. Princess Margaret, who loved parties and took holidays in the Caribbean, was the only family

TOP: Newly married Princess Anne walks up the aisle at Westminster Abbey with Captain Mark Phillips, attended by Prince Edward as pageboy and Lady Sarah Armstrong-Jones as bridesmaid.

BOTTOM: The heroes of the 1974 kidnap attempt at Buckingham Palace following presentation of their gallantry medals.

member who appeared to live like an international millionaire, and she attracted particular resentment. Her marriage had been in difficulties for some time and in 1976 she developed a close friendship with a landscape gardener, Roddy Llewellyn, who was 17 years her junior. She was genuinely fond of this attentive young man, but this was not a relationship that public opinion could condone when the person involved was a married mother and the recipient of public money from the Civil List. The public had come to see her as irresponsible and selfish. Her smoking and drinking, as well as the perception that she did not pull her weight with official duties, created a negative image that she would never escape. She was to live the remaining quarter-century of her life somewhat in the shadows.

The Queen became embroiled in a constitutional crisis on the other side of the world when, in 1975, the Australian Prime Minister Gough Whitlam was dismissed by the country's Governor-General. The latter functions on Her Majesty's behalf as a ceremonial Head of State, but with a crisis of confidence in the Government, the Governor-General has the constitutional right to remove a failing Prime Minister. Had Australia been a republic with a president, that person would have done the same thing. The matter did not involve the Queen, but she got a good deal of blame from those opposed to this move. Republicanism in Australia suddenly blossomed and pundits predicted that the monarchy would disappear, perhaps even by the Jubilee year of 1977. Her Majesty's attitude was, and remains, that it is for the people of the Dominion to decide whether or not they wish her to remain – and more than 35 years later, despite persistent predictions that an Australian republic is imminent, she is still the country's Head of State.

The Queen visited the USA in July 1976 for the country's bicentennial celebrations. She danced at a White House ball and toured Bloomingdale's store in New York but, more significantly, she also went to Boston, the 'Cradle of the Revolution'. In melting summer heat, she stood in front of the Old State House to make a speech praising the vision and ability of America's founding fathers. She raised a laugh by saying how surprised they would be to know that a descendant of George III was standing on that spot. She was an ideal guest for the nation's 200th birthday party – a familiar and respected figure who could be relied upon to behave with dignity, to say and do the right things and to heighten the sense of occasion.

The schedule was unforgiving. For almost a week she was required to attend eight or nine events every day, beginning at around 10 a.m. and going on until midnight, with only two short breaks and two hours or so off in early evening. At a series of receptions she had to meet, greet and shake hands with over a thousand people at a time. Her hosts were rarely unimpressed. Henry Kissinger said that she had 'made a unique and enormous contribution to Anglo-American relations.'

The Queen toured the Commonwealth during the 1970s, her visits a celebration of her Silver Jubilee. These were divided into two journeys. One was in spring, the other in autumn, ensuring that she would be home for the summer and the national celebrations there. Her travels covered an astonishing 56,000 miles altogether. They were intended to show her overseas peoples their sovereign and to reassure the Dominions that Britain – which had shifted its focus to Europe by joining the Common Market in 1973 – had not cut its links with them. Since, to a large extent, this is precisely what it had done, the sentimental ties of monarchy were almost all that was left to bind the former British Empire.

There was no doubting the Queen's enthusiasm for the Commonwealth, or the pleasure her visits gave. At home, where inflation and unemployment were rampant, it was seen by the Government as inappropriate that major celebrations should mark the 25th anniversary of her accession. Although she had become Queen in February, the anniversary would be commemorated in June with a thanksgiving service at St Paul's Cathedral. The momentum for this built up slowly, because it was not known how

TOP: In the Royal Box for the Gala Silver Jubilee Performance at the Royal Opera House, Covent Garden, May 1977.

MIDDLE LEFT: Dancing with President Gerald Ford following a White House banquet, 1976.

BOTTOM LEFT: The Queen at home in Windsor, 1977.

BOTTOM RIGHT: Princess Margaret with Lord Colin Tennant, awaiting the Queen's arrival in Mustique, 1977.

the public would react. There had not been a Jubilee since that of George V in 1935. People did not know what it meant, how it should be celebrated or what it would involve. In a reprise of the attitude that had been seen at the time of the Queen's wedding 30 years earlier, the Government had misread the public mood. Thinking that at a time of national austerity there was no excuse for expensive celebrations, it had not realised how much the British people wanted something to celebrate. As in 1947, so in 1977: the public turned out in droves, elated by the very fact that their recession-hit country was having a party.

Her Majesty made extensive tours of Britain to ensure that the atmosphere of celebration was spread as widely as possible. She was genuinely moved by the reaction of the crowds, which greeted her with undisguised joy. Regardless of the vicissitudes of the time and of people's views on the cost of maintaining the Royals, opinion polls throughout the decade had given the monarchy a solid, 75-per-cent approval rating, and even two-thirds of young people were in favour of Britain having a Royal Family.

The fact that she was to tour the United Kingdom meant that the Queen was also to visit Northern Ireland. Its Protestant majority was, and is, among the monarchy's most fervent supporters, but the climate of violence in the Province was such that the Northern Ireland Secretary, Roy Mason, felt it better to cancel. The Queen overruled, telling her Private Secretary: 'Martin, we said we were going to Ulster and it would be a great pity not to.' And so she went, greatly enhancing her popularity – though not with everyone. In the Republic, where her Jubilee was not televised, the Irish Independent sniffed that: 'The British queen's visit to the North is one of the most unwelcome arrangements that the inoffensive woman has ever agreed to.' Nevertheless the reception in Ulster was the most touchingly enthusiastic anywhere. As one of her chaplains put it: 'She could not believe that people had that much affection for her.'

TOP: The Christening of the Queen's first grandchild, Peter Phillips, Buckingham Palace, December 1977.

BOTTOM: The Queen and Prince Philip in the drawing room at Balmoral, February 1977.

The Jubilee itself was celebrated on 7 June 1977. A grey, overcast day that brightened in the afternoon, it was not the test of endurance that the Coronation had been. People slept in the streets all along the processional route from the Palace to St Paul's, and cheered the golden coach just as they had a quarter-century earlier. As always, the splendour of uniforms, liveries, horse-furniture and brass instruments made the event a visual banquet. The Queen dressed in pink and wore one of the turban hats that were a trademark at that time, Prince Philip was in the uniform of an Admiral of the Fleet, and Prince Charles wore that of Colonel of the Welsh Guards. The Cathedral service, attended by the entire Family, was followed by lunch at the Guildhall, after which they returned to the Palace and appeared on the balcony. For millions of her subjects the day was one of local celebration. In countless photo albums there are pictures of longhaired men, and adults and children in flared trousers eating sausages at village fêtes, running in egg-and-spoon races, waving from floats or tangled in maypoles. Both Queen and country seemed blessed

Two years afterwards, as the country was enjoying the sunshine of an August Bank Holiday weekend, news came that Lord Mountbatten had been murdered while on holiday in the west of Ireland. He had regularly spent his summers there and was known, and loved, by local people. He had disregarded the danger of terrorist attack, feeling that he was too old to be a target. He was blown up by a bomb placed on a small fishing boat in which he was leaving harbour. The explosion killed him, as well as one of his twin grandsons, his son-in-law's mother and a local boy. The Queen and Prince Philip were on a private tour of the Loire chateaux in France. They returned at once, and Mountbatten received a state funeral in London. The last Royal image of the decade was that of a coffin drawn on a gun-carriage by sailors processing through the streets and the Family, grief-stricken but as stoical as always, bidding farewells.

TOP: The balcony at Buckingham Palace during the Silver Jubilee celebrations, June 1977.

BOTTOM: The funeral of Lord Mountbatten, September 1979.

CHAPTER SEVEN: 1980 – 1990

❧

THE ROYAL
REVIVAL

Trooping the Colour is a spectacular ceremony staged every year on the second Saturday in June to celebrate the sovereign's official birthday. In 1981, the event was going entirely to plan, as it always does. The Mall was lined with Union Flags, hanging limp. The crowds were happy in the June sunshine, standing patiently behind the crush-barriers. Policemen were stationed at intervals, the sunlight glinting on their silver helmet-plates. The Guardsmen, also precise widths apart, stood ramrod straight. A husky, aristocratic voice shouted the order: 'Royal Salute! Pree-sent . . . Arms!' The Queen loved this occasion. She had known it all her life.

She was in the uniform of the Welsh Guards, whose Colour was to be trooped that day and was riding her mare, Burmese, who had served with her at this event since 1969. Burmese moved at a steady pace. There was no hurry. Her Majesty was almost at the Admiralty Citadel, where the procession turns right into Approach Road and the parade ground, when a succession of shots rang out.

On duty at that corner was Lance Corporal Galloway of 2nd Battalion, Scots Guards. Like other 'street liners', his function was to present arms as Her Majesty went by. He later recalled in the laconic language of a military report: 'There was a noise which I thought was the crowd clapping; then I recognised it was gunfire. I turned round and saw a man pointing a gun at the Queen, and as I turned he fired the last shot. The crowd was shouting and he was being pushed forward. I leaned across the barrier, grabbed him by the hair and pulled him into the Mall [where police took hold of him. Then] I returned to my position.'

Onlookers saw the Queen deviate from her normal, straight-backed posture only to pat her horse's neck in a calming gesture. Her Majesty later said that the animal had become nervous not because of the shots but owing to the sudden activity as other riders closed in protectively around her. The procession moved onto the parade ground as if nothing were amiss, the ceremony went ahead entirely as usual, and she rode back along the Mall when it was over.

The man responsible had been armed only with a starting pistol, which he fired six times. The Queen had not been in danger, though naturally no one could have known that. The perpetrator, Marcus Sarjeant, had sought to become 'the most famous teenager in the world' through this act. He would have used a real weapon and live bullets had he been able to obtain them. Sentenced to five years in jail, he was to write to the Queen to apologise. He received no reply.

It had already been a dangerous year for world leaders. In March, another disturbed young man had shot Ronald Reagan in Washington. The President was hit by ricochet, the bullet passing within an inch of his heart. In May, Pope John Paul II had been hit four times by a would-be assassin's bullets in St Peter's Square. His attacker, a Turk called Mehmet Ali Ajca, had originally decided to shoot the British monarch but, on learning that this was a woman, had sought another victim. In the same month a bomb had exploded in the normally peaceful Shetland Islands while the Queen was opening the new oil terminal at Sullom Voe. The device caused damage in a part of the premises Her Majesty was not visiting, but this was still seen as an assassination attempt. As a result of the incident in the Mall, police were ordered on all future occasions to face into the crowd, not away from it.

The events that defined the 1980s almost all occurred early in the decade: the Falklands War, in which the Queen's second son participated; the race riots in British cities and the violence that characterised the miners' strike of 1984. As in the 1970s, the news images that filled television screens were often ugly and disturbing – pickets, riots and burning buildings – but this time there were also burning warships, hit by Exocet missiles. Terrorism continued to be a plague – one bomb exploding within earshot of the Queen and killing members of her Household Cavalry.

Once again, it was the House of Windsor that provided the brighter moments, the excuse to celebrate. The Queen's two eldest sons were married in ceremonies that were watched by television audiences throughout the world, and the women they brought into the

RIGHT: Princess Diana and Prince Charles leaving St Paul's Cathedral as man and wife, July 1981.

Family changed public perceptions of royalty for a generation. There were Royal grandchildren at frequent intervals: Zara (1981), William (1982), Harry (1984) and Beatrice (1988).

Prince Charles's wedding to Lady Diana Spencer in July 1981 was the focus for a huge outpouring of public sentiment. The Prince had reached the age of 32 without marrying and his father, who had married at 26, told him pointedly that unless he made a decision soon there would be no suitable brides left. Charles had always been of an indecisive nature and both his parents wanted not only to see him settled but also to have the succession secured. The Prince had had no shortage of girlfriends, most of them from upper-class English backgrounds. One of these, Lady Sarah Spencer, had a younger sister whom Charles met at a shoot on her family's estate.

Even as a teenager, Diana projected considerable charm, humour and personality. She was athletic, tomboyish, affectionate and possessed a winsome beauty that had not yet quite blossomed. Her family was well-versed in the ways of the Court (her grandmother was a close friend of Charles's grandmother) and she had lived for some years on the Sandringham Estate, thus enabling the press to suggest that she was 'the girl next door'.

For months during the winter of 1980–1981, speculation mounted that the 19-year-old was going to marry Charles. She was followed in the street by press photographers and endured endless media attention. Her trademark shyness, her habit of keeping her head demurely lowered, peering at the world through falling blond locks, made her an instant icon.

In theory, Diana was a highly suitable future queen. Her appealing modesty and her patent affection for children suggested that she would win the nation's affection with ease (she did) and slip comfortably into a life of public duty (she didn't). Charles proposed during a dinner, and allowed her to consider her answer for some weeks while she made a trip to Australia. Their engagement was announced after her return, on 24 February 1981. The wedding date was set for 29 July

TOP: The Royal Family in St Paul's Cathedral for the wedding of Prince Charles and Lady Diana, 29 July 1981.

BOTTOM: The happy couple during their honeymoon at Balmoral.

1981, and a public holiday was declared. The Queen was both happy and relieved. Diana seemed to 'tick every box'.

The wedding was a glorious occasion. Held at St Paul's – Prince Charles's choice of setting – it was a magnificent set-piece of music, architecture and costume. The groom was in the dress uniform of a senior naval officer, the bride – on whom the watching millions focused their attention – wore a dress of white silk taffeta with a train 25 feet long. Its design had been a closely-guarded secret and it was not seen until she emerged from her coach at the cathedral steps. The day's most memorable moment occurred later when, on the Palace balcony, the bride and groom kissed in front of cheering crowds. The service was the most popular Royal event since the Coronation. Some 600,000 people waited in the streets to see the procession, and 3,500 were in the Cathedral. A truly staggering number – 750 million – watched it on television throughout the world.

Charles and Diana were not, however, as well matched as everyone had been led to believe. The gap in their ages was much greater than the 12 years that separated them. He had always been old for his age. A product of the 1950s and 1960s, there had never been a time when he embraced youth culture, he has never cared for rock music and has never dressed like a member of his age group. He and Diana seemed more like a middle-aged father and his teenage daughter than husband and wife.

She did not share his love of opera and high culture, nor did she like his friends, who shared his conservative tastes. She demanded a level of attention that he was not accustomed to giving anyone, and she became strident, moody and argumentative. No one, she complained, gave her the guidance necessary to fulfil her role. She was expected to accustom to a world of state banquets, speech-making and inspection of troops without anyone showing her properly how it was done. All this was understandably intimidating for a nursery-school assistant, even one with an aristocratic background. Her criticism was unfair. Charles was often touchingly concerned about the pressure to which

RIGHT: Diana relaxes into her role as Princess of Wales.

she was subjected. Courtiers were on hand to explain what was necessary (she saw them instead as always telling her what to do). Her parents-in-law, under no illusions that life would be difficult, stood ready to help her should she ask, though effective communications were somehow never established between them. Help was not consistently given – all those around her were busy – and she was expected to learn more quickly than she perhaps felt was reasonable.

Diana had been used to all the freedoms of a well-off young woman in London. She simply could not come to terms with the restrictions of living within the Royal Household – having her life planned for months or even years in advance, being accompanied everywhere by a protection officer. Having a more impulsive nature than the members of her husband's family could ever have afforded, she felt trapped. At the end of that year the princess, who found it increasingly hard no longer to be able to run ordinary errands, was photographed going from her home at Highgrove to buy sweets. She was sufficiently upset by this unrelenting attention for the Queen to call a conference of newspaper editors and request a gentler approach. She was persuasive and reasonable, but when asked by the editor of the *News of the World* why the princess could not 'send a servant to buy her Fruit Gums', Her Majesty retorted: 'That's the most pompous thing I have ever heard.'

The cracks in her marriage did not appear at once, and for several years the Royal Family enjoyed a level of positive press interest that was tantamount to a honeymoon. Since her engagement, Diana had had something of a makeover. With advice and assistance from the fashion press and from stylists, her clothing, hair and make-up became steadily more sophisticated. With her statuesque build and photogenic features, she had everything necessary to be a fashion leader. That she also smiled readily and had a genuine way with people (she spoke to strangers with more spontaneous warmth than the other Royals) made her yet more popular.

When in March 1983 she and her husband visited Australia, they

TOP: The Royal Family attending the Braemar Highland Games, September 1981.

BOTTOM LEFT: A tickle from mummy makes Prince William laugh, December 1982.

BOTTOM RIGHT: The Queen Mother holds Prince William at his Christening in Buckingham Palace, August 1982.

took with them the nine-month-old Prince William. It was a joint decision – though Diana got the credit – and proved immensely popular with Australians. It was believed, erroneously, that she had brought him against the Queen's wishes. Nevertheless, the days when royal infants were left at home while their parents went on official tours were clearly over. This change was seen as evidence that Diana had brought a greater humanity to the House of Windsor. Yet it had also become apparent that Diana would not easily fit into the routine of the Royal Family.

Diana admired the Queen enormously and said so often. She was impressed by the monarch's stamina and unflagging devotion to duty, but she did not want to emulate it. She committed numerous small gaffes, arriving late for meals, deciding to go to bed in the midst of an evening when guests were present, and using ill-health and, especially, headaches to avoid official duties. Although she was both loyal and enthusiastic regarding the charities she took up, she never learned the lesson that Royalty cannot do things – or cancel things – on impulse. The Queen had little sympathy with Diana's protestations. She was to refer to her daughter-in-law as 'that impossible girl'.

There had been many other preoccupations for the Queen. In April 1982, Argentine forces suddenly seized the Falkland Islands, a British dependency in the South Atlantic to which they had long laid claim. The government in Buenos Aires expected a cheap victory, assuming that a nation 8,000 miles away would not – or could not – fight to recapture the islands. They had seriously underestimated the determination of Prime Minister Margaret Thatcher. While America tried to settle the dispute peacefully, the toughest members of the British Armed forces – marines, paratroops, Gurkhas – began the long voyage southward in a hastily assembled naval task force. The Queen's second son, Prince Andrew, was a Sub-Lieutenant aboard HMS *Invincible*. He had recently qualified as a pilot on Sea King helicopters but, although his skills were certainly required, the Ministry of Defence had initially given him an administrative job out of harm's

TOP: Prince Andrew meets the crowd that gathered to greet HMS *Invincible* on her return from the Falklands, September 1982.

BOTTOM: The Queen, Prince Philip and Princess Anne with Prince Andrew aboard HMS *Invincible* in Portsmouth, September 1982.

way. It was the Queen who insisted that her son should take the same risks as any of the other naval pilots in the fleet.

The campaign lasted for 74 days. It cost the lives of 257 British personnel and more than twice that number of Argentines, as well as three local people. Andrew fulfilled the tasks he was set: anti-submarine patrols, evacuating casualties and, most dangerous of all, acting as a decoy to divert Exocet missiles away from task force vessels. His mother, like the mothers of so many other service personnel, avidly and apprehensively watched the television news each day. Once the fighting ended, on 14 June 1982, she was able to speak to Andrew by telephone in the Falkland Islands' capital, Port Stanley, asking him to convey her pride and gratitude to all of those there. When the task force arrived back in Portsmouth, the Queen and Prince Philip were among the thousands waiting to greet them. The Queen's son had been the first of her family line to see action since her father had been at Jutland in 1916.

Less than a month after the task force's return, around 7:15 on the morning of 9 July 1982, Her Majesty awoke at the Palace to find a strange man in her bedroom. He sat on her bed, agitated and rambling, his right hand dripping blood onto the counterpane. He was holding a broken glass ashtray. He spoke to her about his personal problems, which involved complex family relationships. The Queen kept him talking, but pressed a bell that connected with the police control room. Nothing happened. She tried another that linked with the corridor outside. Again, there was no response.

She was not normally alone. Her husband, with official duties that day, had slept elsewhere so as not to disturb her when setting off early. A policeman guarded her bedroom every night, but he had gone off duty at six o'clock as usual. At that time he was replaced by a footman, who was at that moment walking the corgis in the gardens. A maid who might have heard the bell was cleaning in a nearby room. When the man asked for a cigarette, the Queen seized the opportunity by telling him she had none but could find some. Opening the door into the corridor she encountered the maid, who famously exclaimed:

TOP: Prince Andrew with a Lynx helicopter in 1983. He was to serve for 22 years in the Royal Navy.

BOTTOM LEFT: Prince Edward shows his mother around Gordonstoun School where he was Head Boy, July 1982.

BOTTOM RIGHT: Michael Fagan, who broke into Buckingham Palace and reached the Queen's bedside.

'Bloody hell, Ma'am! What's he doing here?' Just then the footman returned and, keeping the visitor calm with promises to find him a drink, led him through a door and grabbed hold of him.

The police arrived about 10 minutes after the first of the Queen's calls. The intruder, Michael Fagan, was an unemployed, 31-year-old schizophrenic. He had, it transpired, visited the palace before, climbing through an open window and taking a bottle of wine.

The public was outraged. The Prime Minister apologised for the lapse of vigilance. Several police officers were abruptly removed from the palace. It was discovered that the alarm the Queen had twice pressed was not taken seriously because it tended to go off by accident.

Her Majesty was much admired for her handling of the situation. She had experienced every woman's nightmare, and had had no idea if Fagan was armed or determined to harm her. Once Fagan had been taken away, she apparently returned to bed and drank her morning tea. A very considerable review of security, needless to say, followed and the officer outside the Queen's door at night was now armed.

For the first time, and for the whole of the 1980s, the Queen's Prime Minister was a woman. Some in the media had predicted that the two ladies would enjoy a warm rapport, for they were not only the same gender but also the same age. Once the working relationship had begun, however, it was widely rumoured that the atmosphere was hostile. Nevertheless, Mrs Thatcher was a devout monarchist and admired the Queen's sense of duty. Her Majesty has always been punctilious in respecting the choice of the electorate. Each was therefore inclined toward willingness to cooperate. It is also worth remembering that Her Majesty was to attend Mrs Thatcher's 70th birthday party, and that she would make her a Baroness – an honour that, according to the Palace, 'would not have been given without the utmost respect for the recipient'.

On 23 July 1986, the second royal wedding of the decade took place. Prince Andrew, a career naval officer, married Sarah Ferguson, a young woman he had known as a child.

TOP: The Queen meeting wellwishers at RAF Whittering, June 1982.

BOTTOM: The South Atlantic Campaign memorial service, St Paul's Cathedral, June 1985.

She was the second daughter of a former Household Cavalry major who was polo manager to Prince Charles. The couple sat together at lunch at a Windsor house party during Ascot Week in 1985. Flame-haired and boisterous, Sarah was patently good company for Andrew. They shared a somewhat knockabout sense of humour, and mutual attraction was swift. Their engagement was announced the following March.

This time the wedding was at Westminster Abbey. As befitted a more modest event, things were on a smaller scale: the television audience was 500 million and the bride — who arrived in the Glass Coach just as Diana had done — had a 17-foot-long train. Shortly before the ceremony, the groom was created Duke of York, a title traditionally given to second sons and last held by the Queen's father. At the ceremony, Sarah pleased traditionalists by promising in her vows to 'obey' her husband, not least because this was a phrase Diana had omitted. She was popular with the public, which had taken to using her nickname, 'Fergie', and the Queen liked her, too. They often rode together at Windsor and Her Majesty sometimes referred to her as 'my daughter'.

Yet Sarah somehow could not do anything right. She was sniped at in the press for being too large, too noisy, too free-spending, too undignified. At Ascot in 1987, photographers captured a moment of juvenile horseplay — Sarah and Diana poking, with their umbrellas, the behind of another young woman. The newspapers reacted with annoyance, calling them 'silly, simpering girls'. The Duchess also became infamous for the number of expense-paid holidays she took. For her part, Sarah found herself bored because her husband was at sea for lengthy periods and, like Diana, she found the constant expectations that went with royal status irksome and constricting.

The creeping notion of monarchy as 'just like the rest of us' was seen to embarrassing effect in the case of Prince Edward. With Gordonstoun and a spell in New Zealand under his belt, he wished to attend Cambridge University. Prince Charles had passed into Trinity College despite having results that were modest by Cambridge

TOP LEFT: Andrew and Sarah pose for an official engagement photograph in Buckingham Palace, March 1986.

TOP RIGHT: The Queen Mother and Princess Margaret in the procession from Westminster Abbey to Buckingham Palace following Andrew and Sarah's wedding, July 1986.

BOTTOM: Andrew and Sarah seemed ideally suited as husband and wife.

standards. Edward only just got away with the same trick. His enrolment at Jesus College provoked a protest from other students and objections from the faculty. He was pilloried in the satirical press, even though his tutor was subsequently to say that his mind was impressive.

Edward's troubles were not over. He had been sponsored through Cambridge by the Royal Marines, in which he had enlisted as an officer, a post he was committed to taking up after graduation. Joining the Marines in the summer of 1986, he initially did well in training, but his interests lay elsewhere and he eventually decided to request a discharge. Apart from earning his father's fury, his decision to abandon the course took a great deal of courage, considering the humiliation that he had known would be heaped upon him.

Edward continued to court derision by taking a job as a production assistant with Andrew Lloyd-Webber's Really Useful Theatre Company, despite the fact that he was working for a living and experiencing a closer brush with 'ordinary life' than anyone in his family had known. He naturally wanted to progress to staging his own productions, and an attempt was made with the screening of *It's a Royal Knockout*, a charity fundraising event organised by the Prince and involving his brother Andrew and sister-in-law Sarah as well as Princess Anne. It was modelled on a highly popular television programme, but stuffed with celebrities in a manner that is now commonplace. The event was intended to be slapstick; it raised money for good causes and it was not the Royals — who, in period dress, were team captains — that had to look and behave idiotically, running about and falling over. Nevertheless it was seen as undignified, the press did not like it and the Prince made no friends when he lost his temper with them and stalked out of a press conference.

Whatever the problems caused or endured by her children, Her Majesty remained officially silent. Only Princess Anne's behaviour, it seemed, could be relied upon unreservedly. She was created Princess Royal by the Queen in 1987 to acknowledge her unstinting work for charity, yet for Anne, too, there were dark clouds on the horizon.

TOP: Six of the Queen's Prime Ministers gathered for 10 Downing Street's 250th anniversary — Callaghan, Douglas-Home, Thatcher, Macmillan, Wilson and Heath.

BOTTOM: Commonwealth Heads of Government Meeting, Vancouver, Canada, October 1987.

FOLLOWING PAGES
TOP: Princes William and Harry with Peter and Zara Phillips at Sandringham, January 1988.

BOTTOM RIGHT: The Queen riding with Princess Diana, Sandringham, January 1987.

BOTTOM LEFT: The Queen makes her Christmas Day broadcast from Windsor Castle, 1988.

FAR RIGHT: Princess Anne signs scrolls at the British Apparel Export Awards, Mansion House, January 1987.

CHAPTER EIGHT: 1990–2000

TROUBLED TIMES, TRAUMA AND TRAGEDY

PREVIOUS SPREAD:
Firefighters tackle the
blaze at Windsor Castle,
November 1992.

TOP LEFT: The Queen
addresses the European
Parliament in Strasbourg,
May 1992.

TOP RIGHT: Prince Philip,
the Queen, President
Bush and Barbara Bush,
Washington, May 1991.

MIDDLE RIGHT: The
microphones were set for
President Bush when the
Queen spoke on the White
House lawn, May 1991.

BOTTOM LEFT: French
President Francois
Mitterrand greets the
Queen at the Elysee Palace,
Paris, June 1992.

BOTTOM RIGHT: Charles
and Diana looked further
apart than ever on a trip to
South Korea, November
1992.

In 1992 the BBC released a documentary called *Elizabeth R.* In the year that commemorated the 40th anniversary of her accession, it was thought worthwhile to remind the public what Her Majesty does. The footage was filmed during 1990 and 1991. Viewers watched her hosting a visit by the President of Poland, chatting easily with the Prime Minister at Balmoral, welcoming troops home from the first Gulf War, touring parts of the United Kingdom, and – a note of mild farce – speaking on the White House lawn into a microphone that had not been adjusted after the much taller President Bush had welcomed her. Only her hat and glasses were visible. She retrieved the situation when addressing the US Congress by opening with the words: 'I hope you can all see me today.'

The programme was a great success. It was notable for the mirth, the banter and the sense of fun that the Queen displayed. She seemed to smile more often in the course of this single programme than in four decades of public appearances.

She was going to need a cheerful nature in the months ahead when a book, *Diana: Her True Story*, by the journalist Andrew Morton, was published. The book claimed that Diana had been miserable throughout her married life, that her husband had had an affair with his long-term friend Mrs Parker Bowles, that she suffered from the eating disorder bulimia and that she had a tendency towards self-harm – indeed, that she had attempted suicide by throwing herself down a flight of stairs at Sandringham.

Although these were extraordinary allegations, many people were aware that the couple had grown apart. Even if Morton was an experienced royal correspondent, however, and had access to 'inside sources', how could he have discovered so much that was deeply personal? Morton had, since 1990, been working on a book about Diana. This might have become just another coffee-table ornament had she not authorised others to speak for her. It was claimed that Morton had been given extensive access to Diana's friends, who had described her troubled life, although it seemed unthinkable that anyone from her inner circle would actually speak out so publicly. Only after the Princess's death was it revealed that it was Diana who had provided most of the information.

The Queen was, predictably, horrified. There was a great deal Her Majesty had not known about the state of the marriage. The Windsors are capable of great family feeling . Their unique experience and isolation from others can draw them together so that Christmases, for instance, are boisterous occasions. They do not, however, share their problems and the Queen has a strong aversion to interfering in her children's lives. By the time her son explained the situation to her in 1992, it seemed that divorce was the likely outcome, but the Queen could not countenance this. Not only had she a strong personal belief in the sanctity of marriage, but it was also unthinkable that the heir to the throne – the next Supreme Governor of the Anglican Church – should be separated and publicly labelled as an adulterer. She contemplated the damage to the monarchy with even greater disquiet. The Queen met with her eldest son and his wife and urged that they try to reconcile, at least to buy time. Her firmness cowed Diana.

In that year it seemed the entire façade of royal respectability threatened to come crashing down. In March, Prince Andrew and Sarah Ferguson announced their intention to separate. A matter of weeks later, the marriage of Princess Anne and Mark Phillips, who had been apart since 1989, formally ended. At least with the Yorks there was no apparent animosity. Not only Andrew's naval career but also his newly acquired passion for golf had meant they were too often apart, and Sarah sought diversion. They did, however, remain united by affection for their daughters. Any hope of a reconciliation between them – or the buying of time to spread the burden of bad publicity – was, however, spoiled when in August the *Daily Mirror* printed on its front page a picture of the duchess having her toes sucked by a man identifiable as her 'financial advisor', an American called John Bryan. Other images made it evident that she was topless and that her girls were nearby. The paper sold out within hours. 'Fergie is Finished!'

TOP LEFT: The Queen chats to the commander of her guard of honour in Ottowa, Canada, June 1992.

TOP RIGHT: By June 1992, the Wales's failing marriage was front page news.

MIDDLE LEFT: Trooping the Colour, June 1992.

BOTTOM RIGHT: President Bush explains the game at a baseball match in Baltimore, May 1991.

BOTTOM LEFT: In Malta, the Queen recalled the early days of her marriage, May 1992.

Daily Mail

FRIDAY, JUNE 9, 1992

30p

A desperate cry for help over her loveless marriage

PRINCESS DIANA 'TRIED TO TAKE HER OWN LIFE'

BY NIGEL DEMPSTER

THE Princess of Wales, in the depths of despair at her unhappy marriage, took an overdose of pills in an attempt on her own life.

She then phoned Prince Charles, who rushed a doctor to her side. No serious damage was inflicted. Palace insiders say that the attempt, when the Princess was under severe emotional and psychological strain, was never intended to be more than an agonised 'cry for help'.

The Royal Family and senior Buckingham Palace officials, shocked by the Princess's emotional state, maintained absolute secrecy over the events, said to have taken place six years ago.

Princess Diana herself, with extended medical help, recovered to become the highly-successful public figure she is today.

But the marriage has not been mended and the gulf between Diana and Prince Charles is and and wide. The Princess has seriously contemplated divorce and investigated the possibility of talking to a Prime Chancellor, but has now accepted that her position makes it impossible.

She has told friends she is resigned to being locked into a loveless marriage and so will devote all her energies to charities and good works and, of course, her two sons. She has tried to win her husband back but has accepted that all attempts are doomed to failure.

Dogmors amd officials at the Palace had hoped that the events of the crisis in the royal marriage, and Diana's efforts to solve it, could be kept from the public.

But they have now accepted that details of the Princess's suicide attempt and the news of her psychological depression at the time must become public knowledge.

Next month in America, a new book by the writer Nicholas Davies, Diana, A Princess and Her Troubled Marriage, is due to be published. It gives details of the overdose of paracetamol which the took a number of pills after a blazing telephone row with her husband. It reveals how she lay on the bed in Kensington Palace and called him at Highgrove, their Gloucestershire home, telling him what she had done. He immediately phoned their doctor on another line and had him at the Princess's side within minutes.

Approval

Davies claims that the Palace kept all news of this from Press and public for six years. He learned about it from a source close to the royal couple and does not believe that this would have happened without her approval.

It is not impossible that the Princess is allowing this news to get out, knowing that she has successfully rebuilt her life to the confident position where she is the most-admired woman in Britain after the Queen. She may want her marriage, and her self-esteem is high and she is intensely proud of what she has

Turn to Page 2, Col 2

Princess Diana . . . friends make their concern known

THE UNHAPPINESS BEHIND THE SMILE: SEE PAGES 31-34

trumpeted the press. The Duchess, who was with the Royal Family at Balmoral when the story broke, left there shortly afterwards.

Another tabloid, the *Sun*, published material that had been in its possession for some time. This was the script of a taped conversation between Diana and James Gilbey, a man with whom she was obviously intimate. He addressed her numerous times by the pet-names 'Squidge', or 'Squidgy', and thus the affair was dubbed 'Squidgygate' by the media. It seemed that the conversation had taken place on New Year's Eve, 1989.

And then there were even more revelations. 'Camillagate' was the release in the tabloids of transcripts of a telephone conversation between Charles and Mrs Parker Bowles. Much of the content of this dialogue was highly personal and its publication seemed, for the Prince, an all-but-insurmountable humiliation.

The most vivid in the series of Royal misfortunes took place around mid-morning on 20 November 1992 when an electric light bulb, left on too close to a curtain, started a blaze in the private chapel in Windsor Castle. Soon flames were visible on the roof of the Brunswick Tower. The fire lasted 24 hours, doing immense damage to the buildings on the north side of the castle's Upper Ward. Because these rooms were being rewired, most of the treasures they contained had been removed. Thanks to the quick thinking of staff, almost all the artefacts were saved. Among those who came to the rescue were Prince Andrew, who had been working in the Royal Archives.

This event was a personal tragedy for the Queen, who had driven straight from London on receiving word. Of her five homes this is the one for which she has the greatest affection. Its destruction set the seal on her misery and would prompt the most famous words she had spoken in public since the address on her 21st birthday. There had been no damage whatever to the parts of the castle in which the Queen and her family live. Nevertheless, it was tragedy enough and it was to take five years before the damage was repaired.

But even as clearing up and rebuilding began, the Queen's troubles

TOP LEFT: The Queen inspects the damage after the Windsor fire, November 1992.

TOP RIGHT: St George's Hall was gutted in the fire.

BOTTOM: The restoration finished six months ahead of schedule and £3 million under budget.

multiplied. It was immediately announced by the Secretary of State for National Heritage that the repairs to the castle would be paid for from public funds. The castle, which is not the Queen's personal property but the nation's, had not been insured, and the cost was found to be £37 million. There was outrage that, during a savage recession, the world's richest woman was to be subsidised to this extent. 'When the castle stands it is theirs,' fumed Janet Daley, one of many critical journalists, 'but when it burns down it is ours.'

The Queen was genuinely shocked by this reaction and it only made matters worse when the subject of income tax came to the fore once more. Her exemption from this had been causing increasing resentment, and she knew it was time for change. She was willing, but the matter had not yet been resolved when the Windsor fire began. The announcement within days that both she and Prince Charles would start to pay tax made it look as if she were frightened of the public. Only four days after the fire, she made a speech at London's Guildhall that set the seal on her misery. Memorably she used the phrase *annus horribilis* to describe the previous 12 months, though with characteristic humour she expressed this in understatement: 'This is not a year on which I will look back with undiluted pleasure.' she said. 'In the words of one of my more sympathetic correspondents it has been an *Annus Horribilis*. History will take a more moderate view of the events of this year than contemporary commentators. He who has never failed to reach perfection has the right to be the sharpest critic. No institution, including the monarchy, should expect to be free from scrutiny. It can be just as effective if it is made with a touch of gentleness and understanding.'

This was unprecedented. Although she had sounded vulnerable before ('I shall not be able to bear the burden . . .'), it was the first time she had pleaded for her people's compassion, and it was the nearest she had come to being emotional in any public statement.

The following autumn, while the family was at Balmoral, Buckingham Palace opened to the public for the first time in its

TOP LEFT: The Queen makes her 'annus horribilis' speech at The Guildhall, November 1992.

TOP RIGHT: Prince Philip, Prince Charles, the Queen and Queen Mother on their way to Princess Anne's wedding to Commander Tim Laurence, December 1992.

MIDDLE RIGHT: The Queen's official Rolls Royce cars in Red Square, Moscow, October 1994.

BOTTOM: The Queen leaves a service in the Kremlin's Cathedral of the Assumption, October 1994.

history. Since the dispute over Windsor Castle had ended with Her Majesty receiving most of the bill, the ticket sales for one royal residence would now go to pay for the rebuilding of another. Only the ceremonial areas could be seen, and there would be no question of any family rooms being open. Tickets were expensive, and so were the items in the souvenir shop, but there was no lack of customers.

While this represented a change at home, there were far more significant things happening abroad. The collapse of the Communist Bloc at the end of the 1980s was the biggest change the world had seen since 1945. Once Germany had reunited, the Queen visited Berlin and walked through the Brandenburg Gate before laying a wreath at the monument to those killed while trying to cross the Wall. At home she received visitors from the Eastern Bloc – Lech Walesa from Poland and Václav Havel from Czechoslovakia. One of these eastern visitors, President Boris Yeltsin of Russia, invited Her Majesty – in the course of lunch at Buckingham Palace – to pay a state visit to Russia.

There are two such visits each year, and they take about two years to arrange. It was 1994 before the Royal Yacht dropped anchor in the Neva, the river on whose islands St Petersburg was built. There are reasons for such a long period of preparation. An itinerary has to be worked out, an exercise that involves the palace, the host government and the British embassy. It must be decided in minute detail what Her Majesty will see, the people she will meet and the places she will go. There is also the question of the Queen returning her hosts' hospitality with a dinner at her Embassy, at a hotel or – as was commonplace – aboard *Britannia*. For this event, absolutely everything needed – cutlery, crockery, glassware, tablecloths, menus, and so on – will be provided by the palace. The waiting staff and the chefs will also come from there. A great deal of planning goes into such an operation.

Wherever the Queen is to go, an advance party will investigate. It will work out exactly where she is going and how long it will take to get there – to the minute. She brings her own car and chauffeur, and will be driven slowly so that she can be seen. On her trip to Russia

TOP LEFT: The Queen with Russian leader Boris Yeltsin in the Kremlin, October 1994.

TOP RIGHT: The Queen unveils a statue of the 1991 Derby winner 'Generous', June 1995.

MIDDLE LEFT: Prince Philip and the Queen admire an 18th century royal carriage used by Peter the Great and Catherine the Great, St Petersburg, Russia, October 1994.

BOTTOM: The Royal Family outside Clarence House on the Queen Mother's 95th birthday.

her Rolls-Royce was delivered in advance, but her hosts discovered at the last minute that they had no suitable ramps to unload it. A frantic search of railway sidings, the night before the car was needed, provided what was necessary.

Her staff will visit every place she will stay, measuring doorways and rooms and beds, working out the length of time she will stay in each place, how she will enter and exit, and even taking careful note of the colour schemes. She cannot arrive wearing shades that will clash with wallpaper, with the uniforms of a guard of honour or with the sash and ribbon of an order with which she is to be invested

Meanwhile, at the start of each year while she is at Sandringham, she will begin the extensive reading that is necessary for the visits she will make. She works her way through books, articles, reports – anything her staff feel will help her grasp the essence of the place and the people she is going to meet. The making and fitting of the clothes she wears will have begun at least a year ahead. As well as avoiding certain colours, her dressmakers will look for ways of paying compliment. This can be done by incorporating the colours of the national flag, or more commonly by having a decorative pattern that incorporates an indigenous flower.

The Queen also takes with her a number of travel essentials: Malvern water, which she drinks every day; chocolate mints; Dundee cake; Earl Grey tea; her personal kettle; a thermos; a hot water bottle and pillows (how many people cannot sleep comfortably away from home?); barley sugar to ward off travel sickness; and her own soap. Everything is transported in distinctive blue trunks. Yellow labels are fixed to the Queen's, to mark them out from those of others in her party. There are also hatboxes, jewel-cases and other items. A specialist servant, the Travelling Yeoman, is tasked with looking after the luggage. One of his problems is disembarking the trunks after she has arrived at her destination, and getting them to the embassy, or the hotel, *before* she reaches it.

If she is staying in a hotel, which is not uncommon, an entire

TOP: Princess Diana, Prince Harry and Prince Charles meet Prince William's House Master at Eton, Dr Andrew Gailey, September 1995.

MIDDLE RIGHT: Prince Philip receives a hongi (traditional Maori welcome) in New Zealand, October 1995.

BOTTOM RIGHT: Nelson Mandela greets the Queen as she arrives in Cape Town, March 1995.

BOTTOM LEFT: The Queen wearing a cloak of Kiwi feathers by the Prince of Wales Geyser at Rotorua, New Zealand, October 1995.

floor will be rented for her and her suite. When, in 1968, she visited Vienna, 40 rooms of the Imperial Hotel were allocated to her. She and Prince Philip occupied seven of them, their staff – typically there would be about 30 travelling with them – and their baggage had the rest. Her Majesty's rooms were refurnished specially. Not for her the bland decor and reproduction paintings seen even in expensive hotels. Her suite was filled with baroque treasures that had belonged to the Empress Maria Theresa, brought out of government store. A direct telephone link was installed with Buckingham Palace, and two guards, quite apart from the Queen's own protection officers, were stationed outside all day and night.

While the Queen's staff plan for every contingency, there are sometimes mishaps. Notorious in the annals of royal travel was her state visit to Morocco in 1989, when the king kept her waiting for over three hours in the heat on her arrival.

Two of her visits during the 1990s were of special significance. In Russia she stayed in the Kremlin, a fortress in the centre of Moscow whose very name evokes chilling memories of the Cold War. Before the revolution it was a place of pilgrimage and Her Majesty participated in a service, with the Orthodox Metropolitan Church of Moscow, in one of its several cathedrals.

She had several reasons for finding this a moving experience. The Romanovs, the murdered family of the Tsar, were relations of hers, and she had heard stories of them from her grandmother and from Lord Mountbatten.

There was another bright moment the following year when she visited South Africa, for the first time since 1947. After long years of defiant isolation, the country had abandoned its apartheid government, become a fully democratic state and been readmitted to the Commonwealth. Nelson Mandela was now president, and he and the Queen had a genuine and unmistakeable mutual admiration. She found him refreshingly unlike any world statesman with whom she had previously dealt. She brought with her, and gave him, the Order of

TOP: The Queen smiles with President Nelson Mandela outside De Tuynhuys, the president's official residence in Cape Town, March 1995.

BOTTOM: The Queen Mother and her daughters on the balcony at Buckingham Palace to celebrate the 50th anniversary of VE Day, May 1995.

Merit, an award that is entirely in her personal gift and independent of government recommendation. The only other non-British recipients in recent times have been those two other popular saints of the 20th century – Albert Schweitzer and Mother Theresa.

In the middle of the decade came the 50th anniversary of the end of the Second World War. This was to be a national celebration, at which the Royal Family – and especially the Queen and Queen Mother – were to be highly visible. It was speculated by those planning the event, that, with the unpopularity of the monarchy, the turnout would be low. But, just as with every time this argument had been used since 1947, the pessimists were proved wrong. Hyde Park had been envisaged as the venue, but was felt perhaps to be too big and thus liable to look embarrassingly empty. On the day itself – 8 May – it was packed. This celebration, in any case, focused on the older generation of the Royal Family, and not on their errant offspring. It reminded the public of the service given to the country by the Queen and her mother. The Queen Mother, with her two daughters, appeared on the palace balcony just as they had a half-century earlier and, in the course of the celebrations, they sang with the rest of the audience the wartime songs. When one of those who led the singing, Cliff Richard, complimented the Queen Mother on remembering the words, she answered: 'We've been rehearsing this for about three weeks.'

In November 1995 the last nail was put in the coffin of the Wales's marriage. The previous year, Charles had participated in a televised interview with the broadcaster Jonathan Dimbleby, who had written a magisterial biography of the prince. The picture it gave of Charles's parents – his father a no-nonsense bully and his mother preoccupied with affairs of state – was not a flattering one. Charles was presented as an extremely well-meaning man doing his best for the country and the monarchy. The programme was largely remembered, however, for the simple fact that he admitted adultery on television.

Now Diana hit back with the same weapon. She too gave an interview, to the BBC current-affairs programme *Panorama*. No one

TOP: Charles, Diana and their sons are joined by the Queen and Prince William's godparents for his confirmation, March 1997.

BOTTOM: Princess Diana's brother, her sons and her ex-husband watch her coffin pass by.

could argue that she was not a wronged woman, but she too admitted adultery, with a Household Cavalry officer. She went on to say that she did not think her husband was fit to become king. For her mother-in-law, Diana's TV appearance was a problem that could simply not be ignored. It had even happened on the Queen's wedding anniversary. The day after the programme was broadcast, Her Majesty wrote to Diana and Charles asking them to divorce. Damage limitation had to begin at once before this situation could further threaten the monarchy. Their separation became final eight months later.

Then, on 31 August 1997, came the car accident in Paris in which Diana died. The Royal Family was at Balmoral. It was as great a shock to them as it was to the rest of the world, but this did not show and was not perceived. Balmoral is a holiday home and, while they are there, the family are not often seen outside the walls of the estate. Had they been in London, they would perhaps have made some public gesture. As it was, they remained out of sight. This did not mean they were not grieving, merely that they could not be seen to be doing so. Public opinion was as fickle as always. Throughout that summer there had been much adverse press comment on the princess's lifestyle as she was photographed romping in the Mediterranean, and her flirtation with a man many considered unsuitable had lost her much credibility.

Suddenly it seemed deeply churlish to have begrudged her the right to happiness.

Such was the outpouring of grief that any negative attitude was seen as insensitive and spiteful. Tributes piled up in such numbers that florists could not keep up with demand.

They carpeted the ground outside the palaces where she had lived. In this atmosphere of hysteria the truth did not matter, only people's perceptions. The princess's parents-in-law had cast her out. They had then compounded their cruelty by failing to mourn.

The Queen's attitude was that the death was a family tragedy and that it should be dealt with in private. Her greatest concern was for

LEFT: The Queen, Prince Philip and the Queen Mother leaving Wesminster Abbey after Princess Diana's funeral.

her grandsons, who had to be protected, and that normality should be preserved as much as possible. To an extent that many people considered inappropriate, this involved business as usual — carrying on with the sporting pursuits of the season apparently as if nothing had happened. It was days before a mounting tide of press outrage, demanding that Her Majesty 'come back and lead the nation's mourning' convinced her to return. She was roundly blamed for failing to have a national flag flown at half-mast from the palace, even though *no* flag other than the Royal Standard was ever seen there. One could not argue points of protocol at such a time, so she authorised the change that opinion demanded.

Having permitted the Union Flag to be hoisted in commemoration of Diana's death, the Queen has allowed it to be flown over the palace ever since when she is not in residence.

Returning to London the day before the funeral, the sight of her car coming down Constitution Hill caused spontaneous applause from the large crowd in front of the palace. The 'walkabout' immediately undertaken by the Queen and her husband to examine the flowers and read inscriptions began to repair the damage. She made a broadcast inside the building, through whose windows the crowd could be seen.

The princess's death was a tragedy, but the Queen's quiet dignity was not as inappropriate as some believed, although the monarch was seen to have learned important lessons. The Royal Household had established a committee called the Way Ahead Group to review their strategy of visits and functions so as to make them more responsive to public expectations. The palace set up its own website and the Queen has subsequently appeared on Facebook. She has since been seen visiting a pub, being shown round the set of *Eastenders* and attending rehearsals for a West End production of *Oklahoma*. Those who think this evidence that Her Majesty has 'turned over a new leaf' are mistaken. These are things she has always done. She has certainly been in pubs before, and she knew *Oklahoma* very well since she had been taken to see it by Philip during her courting days.

RIGHT: The Royal Family leaves the thanksgiving service at Westminster Abbey for the Queen and Prince Philip's 50th wedding anniversary, November 1997.

A grief of a different kind visited the Royal Family with the decommissioning of *Britannia* – on grounds of expense, because the cost of modernisation was too great – in 1997, after it had travelled more than a million miles. *Britannia* had become closer to the hearts of the Royal Family than any piece of machinery could be expected to do. Linked with her father, because he had approved its design before his death, and launched more or less as she became Queen, they had begun their official careers together. It was associated with numerous holidays and royal honeymoons as well as with official visits. In port it served as a floating embassy, the venue for numerous receptions.

More importantly, it was a sort of seagoing Balmoral – a home in which the Queen could entirely relax because it offered such privacy. With miles of ocean all around her it was safe from the lenses of press photographers. Anyone could be expected to show sadness at losing such a familiar friend.

A few months before the end of the 1990s – on 19 June 1999 – the Queen's youngest son was married. This was an event in stark contrast to the extravagant occasions of the previous decade. Now that every one of his siblings was divorced, it seemed perhaps inappropriate to draw too much attention to Prince Edward's wedding. It took place at St George's Chapel in Windsor Castle. The groom, now created Earl of Wessex, arrived on foot with his two brothers from their home in the Upper Ward a few yards away. He wore no uniform, merely a tailcoat. The bride, Sophie Rhys-Jones, a 34-year-old who worked in public relations, likewise had no train, and arrived in a simple but sleek white suit-dress. The guests were brought in by minibus.

Apart from the grandness of the building itself, this could have been the wedding of any young middle-class couple of prosperous parentage. One of the guests, the actor Anthony Andrews (who reported that the Queen did the twist at the celebrations afterwards), commented: 'You felt that you were part of a family occasion, rather than a state one.' A reminder that, whatever their problems, the Royal Family are just like us. They get over their difficulties and carry on.

TOP: A few tears were shed while saying goodbye to Britannia.

BOTTOM: Prince Edward marries Sopie Rhys Jones at Windsor Castle, June, 1999.

A 21st Century Monarch

The official celebrations for the start of the new millennium were to take place on New Year's Eve, 1999 at the Millennium Dome in Greenwich. The Queen and Prince Philip, who would not normally have been in London, had agreed to attend, sitting next to Prime Minister Tony Blair and his wife, Cherie. At midnight, were obliged to stand up, join hands and take part in singing 'Auld Lang Syne'. They are not given to demonstrative public behaviour, and there was certainly some awkwardness. Blair himself recorded in his memoirs that: 'I don't know what Prince Philip thought of it all, but I shouldn't imagine it's printable. I suspect Her Majesty would have used different language but with the same sentiment.' Shortly afterwards they escaped to Sandringham.

A more successful celebration, in August 2000, was that of the Queen Mother's 100th birthday. The biggest event, in a series of commemorations, was held on Horse Guards Parade. Organised by Major Michael Parker, a military impresario responsible for innumerable tattoos, it involved the charities of which she was patron, the regiments with which she was connected and a wealth of other groups, organisations, representatives – and animals. There were chickens and cattle in the procession that passed in front of Her Majesty, for every aspect of her life was to be reflected. On the day itself – 4 August – there was some amusement when she received from her daughter the customary message of congratulations sent to every centenarian: 'The Queen is much interested to hear that you are celebrating your one hundredth birthday, and sends you warm congratulations and good wishes.'

For the Royal Family, as for the rest of the world, the new century effectively began on 11 September 2001 with the terrorist attacks in New York and Washington. The family was at Balmoral, and followed the events on television. Among the dead there were many subjects of the Queen, and she shared in full the general sense of shock and grief. The events of that day heralded the advent of a new age of international terror just as the old era of more local terrorism was

PREVIOUS SPREAD: The Queen inspects her guard of honour outside the Canadian Parliament in Ottowa, July 2010.

TOP: 'Auld Lang Syne' with Tony and Cherie Blair at the Millennium Dome, January 1 2000.

MIDDLE: The Royal Family on the balcony at Buckingham Palace for the Queen Mother's 100th birthday, August 2000.

BOTTOM LEFT: The Queen Mother arrives at Buckingham Palace on her 100th birthday.

BOTTOM RIGHT: Mother and daughter share a laugh as two male streakers race past at the Epsom Derby, June 2000.

ending. With the Good Friday Agreement, peace had largely returned to Ulster and now those who protected the Queen had to look for danger from a new direction.

Amid the climate of fearful disbelief that followed the attacks of 11 September, there were some symbolic gestures the monarch could make. She authorised, on the day of mourning, the playing of 'The Star-spangled Banner' during the changing of the guard at Buckingham Palace. In attendance were Prince Andrew and the US Ambassador, while outside the railings were crowds of expatriate Americans. The Queen visited New York, went to Ground Zero, attended a commemorative service, and awarded the city's dynamic mayor, Rudolph Giuliani, the KBE for his leadership during the crisis.

Even as the world mourned the victims of 9/11, plans were forging ahead for a far happier event, the celebration of the Queen's Golden Jubilee in the summer of 2002. This time more than ever, in view of the drubbing the Royal Family's reputation had endured in the previous decade, official opinion was hesitant about the scale of celebrations. Would a large event be too ambitious? Would The Mall look embarrassingly empty if not enough people turned out? It became obvious during the spring of 2002 that momentum was building, and it was decided that there would be a four-day commemoration, spread over a weekend at the end of May and beginning of June. There would be a procession to St Paul's, a thanksgiving service, a balcony appearance, fireworks – all the things that people hope for and expect.

Just as the Jubilee plans were moving into top gear, the Family was struck by tragedy. Princess Margaret had been an increasingly shadowy presence in public life since the traumas of the 1970s. Recently her health had also been failing. She had suffered bronchitis and laryngitis. A smoker, like her father, she had – like him – undergone a lung operation. In 1998 she had a stroke. She subsequently, and badly, scalded her feet in a bath. She had a second stroke. By the time she was seen on the occasion of the Queen

RIGHT: Princess Margaret's son and daughter, Viscount Linley and Lady Sarah Chatto, stand with the Queen at their mother's funeral.

Mother's 100th birthday she was a pitiable figure, confined to a wheelchair, expressionless and apparently speechless, her eyes hidden by sunglasses. She was in great pain, and confided to a friend that she longed 'to join Papa'. On 9 February – three days after the anniversary of his death – she did. Following a third stroke she was taken to hospital, where she died.

The Queen Mother, too, was visibly declining. She refused to be defeated by age or infirmity, insisting on entertaining guests or making visits despite having to walk, slowly and painfully, with sticks. She seemed to keep going entirely by willpower, but then this had always been her defining quality. It had enabled her to lead the monarchy's fight-back after the abdication, to transform her shy husband into a hugely popular king, and to be a mother to the nation during the Second World War. Hitler had called her 'the most dangerous woman in Europe'. Among her former subjects her popularity was limitless. In 2001 her great-grandson William had called on her before going off to university. 'Any good parties, be sure and let me know!' she had allegedly told him. This was among her last recorded statements. It was cherished by the public as evidence of a sparkling sense of fun that combined with an uncrushable spirit. Her last days were spent at Royal Lodge, the home in Windsor that she and her husband had first occupied in the 1920s.

Her last moments came on Easter Saturday, in the afternoon. The Queen, who had been riding in the Park, went at once to her bedside and was there when she died. A million people stood in the streets to see the Queen Mother's coffin pass, or waited for up to nine hours to view her coffin in Westminster Hall.

Despite this national mourning, the Jubilee went ahead as envisaged. Her Majesty made tours of Commonwealth countries, and visited the four parts of the United Kingdom. On 4 June 2002, she travelled with her husband to St Paul's in the Coronation Coach. Over a million waited along the route, on a damp and overcast morning, to see her. The Queen set off from the Palace dressed in sky blue. When

TOP: The Queen Mother's coffin arrives at Wesminster Abbey for her funeral service, 9 April 2002.

BOTTOM: The Queen watches her mother's coffin being taken from Westminster Abbey on its way to Windsor where the Queen Mother was laid to rest in St George's Chapel, Windsor, alongside her husband and Princess Margaret.

she returned, hours later, the weather had changed and so had she, for she was now in pink. As she stood on the palace balcony she could see that, beyond the Victoria Memorial, The Mall was a solid mass of people all the way to the distant Admiralty Arch.

In the sky, far to the east, there were distant specks that grew bigger as the seconds passed. Aircraft in tight formation aligned on The Mall. Now the sound of them caused the crowd to look up. The Red Arrows, the RAF's aerobatic team, shot over their heads with a reverberating roar, leaving a hanging trail of red, white and blue smoke. Ahead of them, the scream of its engines so loud that it drowned even the noise from the thousands below, was the sleek white shape of Concorde. Its sharp nose lifted gracefully as it peeled off and climbed towards the stratosphere. Hundreds of thousands gasped, and then cheered.

The Golden Jubilee was a very different experience from the ceremonial events of 1977. The procession that had followed Her Majesty back to the palace – she and Prince Philip had returned standing up in an open Land Rover – included more than the bands and marching dignitaries that onlookers expected, and the atmosphere was noticeably more informal. The public took away memories of elaborate West Indian carnival costumes, pumping rock music and VC winners travelling in a vintage car. Another change was that members of the Royal Family (though not the monarch herself) had come out of the palace the evening before the celebrations to meet some of those who were sitting all night on the kerbsides. Since the 100th-birthday celebrations for the Queen Mother, it seems there has been a hint of quirky eccentricity in the planning of popular royal occasions. The notion of a rock musician, Brian May, playing 'God Save the Queen' on electric guitar on the roof of the palace that evening (there was a concert for the public in the gardens) was a gesture that captured the imagination of millions around the world.

There have been other celebrations since the Golden Jubilee, and it appears that royal hospitality, always impressive, is gaining an

TOP LEFT: The Gold State Coach carries the Queen to St Paul's Cathedral for the thanksgiving service for her Golden Jubilee, 4 June 2002.

TOP RIGHT: The Gold State Coach is drawn by eight horses but moves no faster than walking pace.

MIDDLE RIGHT: The Royal Family arrives in St Paul's Cathedral.

BOTTOM RIGHT: Front page of the Daily Mail Golden Jubilee special edition, 1 June 2002.

BOTTOM LEFT: Costumed dancers in the parade down The Mall to Buckingham Palace for the Golden Jubilee celebrations, 4 June 2002.

element of imagination too. Already the Queen and Prince Philip had had the notion of celebrating their 50th wedding anniversary with a garden party for other couples who had 'tied the knot' in the year 1947. Even more charming was the Queen's 80th birthday celebration. This, too, was held in the gardens of Buckingham Palace, but the guests were 2,000 children – as well as a host of characters from children's literature and television. A specially written play was put on with a cast of celebrities, entitled *The Queen's Handbag*. In the story, this most famous of Royal accessories is stolen, but is restored to her at the end. 'Oh good,' said Her Majesty, who was also watching the performance. 'I do like happy endings.'

In her eighties, the Queen remains fixed in habit. She spends the year in the same places, doing the same things (though sadly she has had to give up riding). She likes Earl Grey tea, and German wines but not champagne (both she and Prince Philip only pretend to sip it during toasts). She does not eat pasta because the sauces are likely to be messy, and avoids shellfish because of the possible ill-effects. She likes simple food because she has to eat so much elaborate fare on official occasions. Being of a frugal nature, she expects the leftovers from palace meals to be utilised for days afterwards.

She is greatly attached to Windsor, Balmoral and Sandringham. This latter, a Victorian building described – with some justification – as looking like a 'Scottish golf hotel', is the place in which she can come closest to the life of a farmer's wife that she coveted as a girl. Her estate grows commercial crops – such as blackcurrants that end up in Ribena – and she is president of the local Women's Institute, as her mother was before her. Her neighbours and tenants include people whose families she has known through generations.

When at Buckingham Palace – and that is where most of her time is spent – she awakens at 7:30, when her tea is brought. Her dogs are, meanwhile, being walked in the gardens. She breakfasts an hour later, alone with Prince Philip, and reads the *Daily Telegraph*. While she does so, a piper plays outside for 15 minutes. This was a tradition started by

TOP: Concorde and The Red Arrows fly over Buckingham Palace during the Golden Jubilee celebrations, 4 June 2002.

MIDDLE LEFT: Union flags were projected onto the front of Buckingham Palace as fireworks exploded overhead.

MIDDLE RIGHT: Brian May, guitarist with rock band Queen, plays God Save the Queen on the roof of Buckingham Palace.

BOTTOM: Special lighting was used to great effect for the 'Party at the Palace'.

Victoria, and it is not popular with every member of the household. As one author put it, 'it is a sound that inspires no apathy'.

Her mornings are given over to administration. Her Private Secretary brings documents that need her signature, as well as a summary of the day's news and cuttings relating to the Royal Family. She also examines her mail. Her Majesty receives letters at the rate of 2,000–3,000 a day. She glances at the envelopes and chooses 12 or so that she will open. After long years of practice, she has an instinct for finding those that will prove interesting. The ones that need a written reply are passed on to a lady-in-waiting or to her Private Secretary. If the Queen is writing to friends, and she is a regular and disciplined correspondent, she uses green ink to signify that it is a personal letter.

Her audiences take place at around noon, typically last a matter of 10 minutes or so, involving ambassadors, clerics, academics and senior officers. There is not time to deal with any subject in detail, and the Queen's reticence has led some of those she received to confess that keeping the conversational ball in the air was a struggle. As always, however, it is not what she said but the fact that she met with them that is important. She normally lunches by herself, or with Prince Philip if he is not busy with his own duties, in the bow-windowed sitting room that faces towards Green Park. She chooses her meals at the beginning of every week from a list of suggestions prepared by the chef, so she always knows what to expect. After lunch she walks with her dogs in the gardens. She likes to be alone, so staff must stay out of her sight. There follows a brief interlude with the racing papers, and then further business, perhaps involving a visit somewhere. Whatever she is doing, she will have finished before five o'clock so that she can have tea, which is her favourite meal. The miniature sandwiches and Dundee cake are the same every day, as are the scones – which she feeds to her dogs.

If it is Tuesday she will have her weekly visit from the Prime Minister at 6:30, and this will last until about seven o'clock. If she has no evening engagement, she may dine with her husband and then

RIGHT: Standing outside The Woolpack, the Queen watches Emmerdale Post Office go up in flames on the set of the TV series, July 2002.

spend an hour or more with her boxes. She reads every evening a summary of the day's events in Parliament. After that, she will perhaps watch television or work on a jigsaw. She retires at about 11.

The Queen is an extremely accomplished and thoughtful hostess. When she dines with others, she is always served first, yet when she finishes everyone else has their plates cleared away. Experienced courtiers therefore waste no time in talking to their neighbours – there will be time for that afterwards – and concentrate on eating. The Queen is aware of the problem, however, and may well have a salad beside her which she will make a pretence of eating in order to allow the other guests more time.

Those who go to Windsor to 'dine and sleep' – short visits by groups of 10 prominent people that involve staying the night – will find that attention to detail characteristic of royal occasions is evident here, too, and that the Queen is personally responsible for much of it. She will have inspected the rooms in which they are to stay, checking that everything they need has been provided, and she will choose books for their bedside tables. Given an audience of people with whom she has some chance to interact she is far more humorous, vivacious and animated than when merely shaking hands. Given a subject on which to discourse – the castle and its contents – she is lively, anecdotal and entertaining. Apart from a lifetime's association with it, she has seriously studied its contents.

When her guests at Windsor are fellow Heads of State, management of the event will naturally be just as flawless. He Majesty will have taken a great deal of interest in the preparation of St George's Hall for the state dinner, discussing the menu and the flower arrangements and the seating plan long in advance. Once again, the way in which things are done by the Queen and her household sets a standard for other countries.

Ronald Reagan said that: 'The state visit to Britain is one of the high points of any president's term of office' – it is known to have more protocol, more formality, but more splendour and magic

TOP: The Royal Family plays host at Buckingham Palace to the visiting Norwegian Royal Family, October 2005.

BOTTOM: The Prince of Wales and the Duchess of Cornwall in the White Drawing room, Windsor Castle following their wedding, April 2005.

than any other official trip abroad, and they expect it to be highly memorable. Another president, Nicolas Sarkozy of France, dined at Windsor in 2008. Bedevilled at home by a reputation for tasteless ostentation, his visit to the Queen was seen by the French media as a litmus-test of his gravitas. If he could pass muster on this occasion, it was implied, he might gain greater respect at home. In the event, he succeeded. The Queen presented him with a stamp album and they talked about this hobby, for her grandfather had also been an enthusiast.

Where she has some common ground with a guest, the Queen will make the most of it. How she coped with a visit from Nicolae Ceausescu of Romania and his wife (they came in 1978 and he awarded her the Order of Socialist Romania), one cannot imagine, but with a far more welcome visitor, President Reagan, she went riding in Windsor Great Park.

Perhaps to her own surprise as much as anyone else's, the Queen became a fashion icon when Stephen Frears' film *The Queen* was released in 2006. Much of the story is set at Balmoral and Her Majesty, as portrayed on the screen, dresses in the outdoor garments appropriate for a Scottish autumn. A world away from Deeside, amid the sophistication of Manhattan, shoppers wanted this same look. The *Daily Telegraph* announced that the film had caused a run on the Barbour jacket: 'New Yorkers want to dress like the Queen,' announced the paper, 'or, to be precise, they want to dress like Helen Mirren playing the Queen.' The manageress of the company's outlet was quoted as explaining: 'The first thing [customers] say is: "Have you seen *The Queen?*" Then they say they want the jacket that the Queen is wearing.'

The Queen's handbags are much commented upon. She apparently has about 200 of them, which is not surprising in view of the range of outfits she possesses. Whatever she keeps in them it is not money, or a credit card, or a passport. One thing she does carry is an S-shaped hook – the sort one sees in butchers' shops – for hanging

TOP LEFT: The Queen jokes with Prince Harry during the Sovereign's Parade when he passed out at Sandhurst, April 2006 . . .

TOP RIGHT: . . . and gives his brother the same treatement six months later.

BOTTOM: The 2006 Christmas broadcast was filmed at Southwark Cathedral.

her bag on the edge of a table when she is dining.

She will also have glasses, a fountain pen and a make-up case that was a gift to her from her husband when they married. Perhaps she has, in addition, family photographs and keys. She is said also to have crosswords cut out of newspapers, to beguile the time for a few minutes between engagements, and a notebook with information about people she is to meet.

And the Royal Family, too, has moved on. Prince Charles appeared in public with Mrs Parker Bowles for the first time in 1999. Six years later the couple were married in a civil ceremony at Windsor. The Queen and Prince Philip attended the subsequent blessing and hosted the wedding reception at Windsor Castle. The next generation have, despite a certain amount of traditional grooming, had the chance to make their own way. The Queen's grandsons William and Harry both took jobs in the army that were demanding and dangerous and in which their royal status, far from helping them, has been a liability. Both have thus gained the respect of a public that continues to be resentful of privilege.

William has, in any case, been far more free to live a normal life than any of those who preceded him as heir to the throne. Earning his way into university and in the services, he has lived in anonymous flats, washed his own dishes, ordered takeaways, browsed in supermarkets, queued at cashpoints and walked the streets unrecognised, clad in the everlasting, jeans-and-trainers uniform of youth. When younger, he was more often photographed in sweatshirts than in a suit. William's courtship has been in keeping with this spirit of egalitarianism. He met a young woman just as any other student might have done. Once married, he even postponed his honeymoon through having to return to work.

The Queen, who granted permission for him to marry, is aware of how this new generation of royalty fits the spirit of the times. Although William's choice of wife has been dictated entirely by affection, it reflects the pattern in monarchies throughout Europe. In

LEFT: The first of the Queen's grandchildren to marry was Peter Philips, seen here with his bride, Autumn Kelly outside St George's Chapel, Windsor, May 2008.

FOLLOWING PAGE TOP AND BOTTOM: The Queen addresses the General Assembly of the United Nations, October 2010, 53 years after her first UN speech.

this bourgeois age, in which power is in the hands not of aristocrats but of businessmen, Royal Families have allied themselves with the middle class. Young members of the Royal Houses of Spain, Norway, Denmark and the Netherlands have without exception married people who work for a living. Royalty owes its survival to an ability to adapt, to reinvent itself, to remain old-fashioned without being left behind.

Despite her age, the Queen continues to be busier than anyone her years should expect to be, and is actually becoming more so. In 2010 she carried out 444 official engagements, of which 57 were overseas. In 2011, because of her grandson's wedding and her husband's 90th birthday, her diary was even more full. Her historic visit to the Irish Republic in May served to underline both her personal magnetism and her continuing value as a symbol of goodwill. When she laid a wreath at a memorial to Irish patriots, her hosts were deeply touched. 'All Ireland missed a heartbeat,' reported the *Irish Independent*, 'when they saw her take a step back and bow her head.' She won more respect for beginning a speech with some words in gaelic. Her gestures will have been premeditated and her speeches written for her, but the making of them was what counted, and by showing a warm, spontaneous nature during less formal moments, she added a further dimension to Anglo-Irish relations. 'Britain's ultimate diplomatic weapon' indeed.

In July 2009 Her Majesty – like her father King George and her great-grandmother Victoria – instituted a medal bearing her name. The Elizabeth Cross is not, like the others, an award for gallantry. It is given to those whose next of kin have been killed on operations or by acts of terrorism. Perhaps the biggest class of recipients will be the wives of servicemen, and the design is therefore distinctly feminine. A brooch rather than a medal, it has no ribbon and is modest in size.

The Queen's own death is something she has always contemplated with equanimity. Devout in her Christian beliefs, she has no qualms about passing on to what Victoria called 'a more equal world'. Plans for her eventual funeral have been in readiness ever since she came

PREVIOUS PAGE:
The Queen received more than 20,000 cards and almost as many emails on her 80th birthday, 21 April 2006.

TOP: The Queen invited 99 guests who shared her 80th birthday to a special reception at Buckingham Palace, April 2006.

BOTTOM: A kiss for the crowd on the balcony at Buckingham Palace following the wedding of the Duke and Duchess of Cambridge, April 2011.

to the throne, though this is standard for all senior royals. They are updated annually by a committee, and known by the codename 'London Bridge'. (The Queen Mother's funeral arrangements were 'Tay Bridge', and Prince Philip's are 'Forth Bridge'.) Once approved by this, the details are sent to the groups that would be affected: the City of Westminster, the Ministry of Defence and, naturally, the police. This is necessary because of what would be involved: the inviting of Heads of State from all over the world, the need to accommodate the international media, the deployment of troops and the closing off of parts of central London. The Queen's executors need not worry over where she will be buried or what the inscription on her tomb will say. All of that has long-since been settled. She has chosen her coffin, and apparently took great pleasure in fine tuning the arrangements.

Is Elizabeth II the best monarch Britain has ever had? It is difficult to say, for such a judgement must be conditional. There have been others who fitted the spirit of their age and who displayed the qualities necessary to lead the country through difficult times. What cannot be denied is that since the Second World War, Britain's Empire has diminished along with its ability to influence world affairs. This has meant that, to an extent no one could have foreseen, the burden of maintaining national prestige has fallen upon the Queen's shoulders. She has succeeded in carrying that burden for 60 years, and that is a monumental attainment. Her calming influence, her tact and wisdom, her ability to make friends for Britain and to preside over the Commonwealth (an organisation that would almost certainly not still exist were it not for her devotion) have gained for her, and by extension her country, a continuing status. By any yardstick, and in any aspect of her life and work, she is a truly great figure, and those of us who are her subjects will always have good reason to be thankful that we have been New Elizabethans.

TOP LEFT: The Queen's wedding dress was put on display at Kensington Palace as part of her Jubilee celebrations in 2002.

TOP RIGHT: The Duchess of Cambridge and the Queen admire the duchess's wedding dress, on display at Buckingham Palace, July 2011.

BOTTOM: The Queen with Irish President Mary McAleese laying wreaths in the Garden of Remembrance in Dublin during the Queen's historic Irish state visit, May 2011.